GHALIB--- (As I understand him)

(Selections, translation and comments) by

Ziauddin Ahmed

tidylink@yahoo.com

Author: Ziauddin Ahmed

Published 2014

Printed in Pakistan

Cover & Title Design: Xavia Inc

Page Layout: Xavia Inc

Print by Xavia Inc. 2014

www.xaviainc.com

tidylink@yahoo.com

Table of Contents

PREFACE

The classics of any language are a source of enlightenment and enjoyment for the world at large. They become so, on account of their content, diction and style. In any translated version the content may perhaps be presented more accurately than the language, diction or style of the original. However, certain translators have done a commendable job of conveying not only the message but the sweetness of tone and beauty of the text. The two that come to mind are Fitzgerald's -- Rubaiyat of Omar Khayyam, and Ahmed Ali's, anthology of Urdu poetry in his book – The Golden tradition. Being impressed and influenced by them and somehow motivated by the message of heritage, I too decided to try my hands at it, and am attempting to delve on some of Ghalib's philosophical poems, those containing his unique and obscure thoughts. I have also been motivated by the fact that, being an immigrant to another society and culture, one sooner than later, begins to look for the flavour of youth and ones own past heritage.

With the rapid trend of globalization and frequent movement of people, a multi-national atmosphere can now be created anywhere with the import of dress, cuisine and traditions from the four corners of the world. So why should literature be left behind? Further, to keep one's future generations in touch with their roots they should to be exposed to ideas and the richness of their own heritage and past traditions. We, who move to settle abroad should neither expect nor force our children to stay away from the main stream of society. Yet, there is no reason why they should not be informed of their inheritance, its cultural background and moral values. We should not, however, force them to compulsively labour and devote their precious time and energy to pursue ideas in the original tongue. Most young people will take up permanent station here and may never like to return to the land which will probably be as foreign to them as this one once was to us.

English language is rapidly acquiring a universal status and has therefore, been chosen as a medium of choice to communicate with the young. It is worthwhile to reflect upon the fact that what is generally thought to be a generation gap, specially in the East, is no such thing. The gap, if there is any, is in our communication. We may differ in ideas and outlooks yet have a common connection and link through our genes. Let us bridge this gap by talking to our children in the language they are comfortable with. They should be given the opportunity to explore these ideas and the basis of their origination, perhaps thus inculcating a desire to learn the unique and original ideas of the masters of various cultures. This venture is, therefore, an attempt to evoke minds, young and old, to examine things in light of an ever changing world of knowledge, at the same time bearing in mind that the ' original' work of the pioneers cannot be duplicated, only preserved to the best of ones ability.

The importance of original literature can not be emphasized enough, yet 'half a loaf is better than none'. So instead of starving our younger generation and then later being blamed for it, or regretting not having passed it on in essence at least, it is better to 'give them the taste of blood and then leave them hungry'. Therefore, we should be able to provide them a flavor of their ancestral background in some form at least. If their quest is genuine they will find the road to the authentic originality themselves. This is my first hand experience, as my own past has played a major role in nurturing this attempt to reignite the flame. That flame which the elders had tried to kindle in me at a young age, but which the distractions and other pursuits of life kept under cover for a very long time.

My parents too, like many others, had migrated from India to Pakistan at the time of the partition of the subcontinent. Consciously or otherwise they tried to hold on to the traditions of their elders. One of which was that young lads should not be too domesticated by being kept in the household and should be sent away from home for upbringing and education. My father and his brothers were all products of Aligarh, away from their home in Delhi. Boarding schools were either out of reach or inadequate in those early days in Pakistan. So I was shunted off to Lahore, away from Karachi, to live with my great aunt A.R. Khatoon, a famed novelist and author of Urdu literature. Although I hated the experience, yet being of an impressionable age of about nine, must have subconsciously acquired the flavour of the atmosphere and the surroundings.

I do remember sitting around with the ladies of the house after the evening meals and listening to the novel that A.R. Khatoon was writing at the time. It was probably ' chashma'. The Lahore experience did not last long and after about a year or so I was called back to Karachi, perhaps at the insistence of my mother. My father did not get a long life, for a few years later he passed away, or I would surely have been shunted out somewhere else. Prof. Ahmed Ali, an eminent scholar, writer, diplomat, and so much more, was my mother's elder brother, and it was his influence and guidance that we then acquired. He became my ideal and I worshiped him as my hero and took him as my mentor. Well! after having finished with the University came the age of independence and I got engrossed in the pursuits of the glamour of it. It was only after migrating to Canada in 1989 and finding time on my hands that I was woken up to search for the lost moorings. I have been motivated to gather the deeply embedded thoughts and drifting ideas and put them down for posterity, to perhaps lay their hands on and take advantage of them.

With this background in mind I am attempting to present some of Ghalib's poetry and its English translation for you to browse through and perhaps enjoy and appreciate the depth of thought of one of the great thinkers of all times. I may not be able to capture the beauty of the original, as no translation can ever equal it, yet if it narrates the ideas and perhaps the thought process of the genius, it would have fulfilled the underlying purpose. I have thus taken the precaution and titled the presentation, **' Ghalib --- as I understand him',** for his intellect and thought is so deep and sometimes obscure, that different meaning can be drawn by different people. You are free to comprehend him to the extent and depth of your own desire and ability.

In this translation of Ghalib my attempt has been to cover two aspects. First to translate verse into verse. In this I may have drifted a little in its true essence, but I feel that this makes the narration more palatable and attractive. As said earlier a translation can never equal the original, yet make it attractive and perhaps it will motivate the reader to prod along to the end. The second idea is to portray the essence and theme of Ghalib's thoughts, of course only as I understand them. It is also my endeavour to acquaint younger readers of Ghalib with the background in which he wrote and to elaborate the underlying hidden and obscure meaning of some verses, thereby to reveal the extent of depth and emotional experience Ghalib was capable of fathoming, expressing and narrating. Some typical and peculiar personalities of eastern culture and tradition, like 'saqi', 'nauha-gar' etc have been elaborated in the explanations. Phenomena like the special relationship of 'Dil o Jigar', i.e. heart and soul, and 'khoon e jigar', 'blood of the liver', have been commented upon but have been adapted to a more comprehensible diction in English. After every verse a paraphrase or 'tashreeh' has been attempted. The paraphrase can not claim to depict the actual thoughts of the poet, for as said earlier Ghalib is not simple to fathom, and ones own subjective understanding of him would be reflected both in the translation and 'tashreeh'. One other thing to note is that the verses are transcribed in Roman script only and no Urdu version is given. This has been done keeping in mind that many young readers would not be well versed in that language and the content is conveyed phonetically to suggest the rhyme and rhythm alone. Those readers who are interested enough can look up the original divans for greater in depth study through individual effort. The entire venture has been both an interesting and a challenging endeavour because the tradition and language of one culture is not explicitly manageable in another, and however perfect, the translation can never equal the original. How far I have succeeded is for you, the reader, to judge and decide.

Asadullah Khan Ghalib (1797 - 1869) was a poet philosopher of India.

[redacted]

[redacted]

INTRODUCTION

They were times of flux, and the entire world was engulfed in a drastic change. It was an age of transformation for all of mankind. The whole world was in tumult because the change was fundamental in nature. Industrialization was spreading rapidly, and with the advent of the machine age a major sifting and shifting of human values was taking affect. Centuries old and established moulds of culture and morality were being reshaped in the light of the immense impact of the material giant of mass production through machines. Man, who had hitherto considered himself completely under the control of Nature and its rampant laws now began to perceive the power of his own discovery and invention -- the machine. He started to use it to his material benefit and the uplift of his fellow-beings, gaining more self confidence and personal security. The ideas of -- ' work now and be rewarded later ', and that -- ' all labour and effort of each individual was being recorded, to be compensated and acknowledged in another life perhaps' ; were being questioned. The entire basis of human morality came under close scrutiny. The theory and belief of a completely subjugated man, which had been exploited by the dogmatic and myopic view of the clergies of the religious beliefs of all three monotheistic orders, too started to show cracks under critical analysis. Man seemed to feel surer of himself and the fear of the unknown began to recede. The subtle workings of 'Mother Nature' which man could not observe by his naked gaze, he could now examine by a telescope over his head or a microscope under his eye. The 'hows' and 'whys' and his own position in the universe of things started becoming clearer to him with the advancement of scientific knowledge. Some of the greatest men of learning were the outcome of this fundamental readjustment of human thought. Ghalib was one of the front-runners of these independent thinkers.

As the title suggests, this is only an individual's attempt to understand the intellect and genius of Ghalib -- the likes of whom take birth but only once for mankind. A large number of people have been drawn into Ghalib's fold and a great variety of work has been done on the poet. One of the greatest of them in English, has been done by (Prof) Ahmed Ali in his book:

The Golden Tradition -- an anthology of Urdu poetry.

Published by Columbia University Press (ISBN 0-231-03688-4)
The back ground and period of Urdu poetry is most comprehensively discussed and explained in it, along with an unparalleled translation of selected poems from celebrated poets of each period.

Ghalib's ever lasting quality is his depth of human knowledge and philosophy presented in a unique tongue, diction and tradition of his time. The depth of thought and observation have been married in the maturity of language and vocabulary. The result is a vast variety of shades of impressions, giving a new slant every time it is read. Therein lies its perpetual bloom and appeal for all ages. Ghalib's philosophy embodies humanity, hence its universal acceptance and admiration. His maturity and intricacy of style is also evident in his double meaning sentences and stanzas, and above all his pun. eg.

Kayuun Jal Gaya na taab-e rukh-e yar daekh kar
Jalta hoon apni taqat-e didaar daekh kar

Why did I not burn on seeing the heat of her ire
I am jealous of my own ability to bear the fire.

Nukta cheen hai gham-e dil, ous ko sunayae na banay
Kaya banay baath, jehan baath banae na banay

Difficult task is the sorrow of the heart, even her, one can't narrate it to.
What use is there to make ado, where no make ado, will ever do.

Ghalib, in my opinion, was a "progressive Muslim", one who questioned, deciphered, understood and only then submitted to Nature's laws. He did not surrender to the dictates of the dogmatic or the fundamentalist's school of thought. His questioning mind brought him to the zenith of detached self-observation and critical personal analysis. He understood the workings of human nature from outside the shackles of ignorant and dogmatic religious beliefs and practices. For he says:

Hum Mouwahid hain, hamara caish hai tark-e rusoom
Millatain jub mitt gaiyan ajzaa-e imaan ho gaiyan

We are monotheists, our belief is to shun traditions and scribes.
Ingredients of faith flourish with the elimination of sects and tribes.

All original thinkers have a sensitivity about them. They are aware and gain consciousness of phenomena which are beyond ordinary humans and want to share it with the world; only to be rebuffed and ridiculed by conformists and propagators of status quo. Original thought leads to the reality of extreme loneliness and elevated comprehension, and is insatiable by temporary companionships which one seeks in the surroundings. Ghalib's awareness and vision were so acute and penetrating that to preserve sanity he sought some relief. Knowing fully well that exceeding the limit would tilt the balance and lead to addiction and escapism. He has narrated this so aptly by saying:

Bay mae kisay hai taqat ashoob-e aaghahee
Kheincha hai eijz-e hawsala nae khat ayagh ka.

Without wine who has the strength to bear the din of consciousness.
The defeat of courage has drawn a mark, on the rim of the cup's evenness.

And he goes further to stress that:

Mae say gharaz nishaat hae kis roosia ko
Eik Goona baekhudi mujhay din raat chahiaye

Which wretched sinner seeks pleasure from wine.
A deep oblivion, day and night for me, there should be.

A state of oblivion or bliss is sought by man since the beginning of time. It may not be achievable in this mortal life but its search is eternal and has been endowed in human nature. Self fulfillment is one form of acquiring it. Contentment comes in spurts and bliss and satisfaction are temporarily achieved when man puts in his best and whole-hearted effort in exposing the hidden embedded talent, possessed by every individual; thus fulfilling the very purpose of his creation perhaps. The liberation of the trapped treasures of ones nature is every ones desire, but the majority of us are lost and tangled in the achievement of glamour and material glitter of this worldly life. Only some can see the truth beyond its physical garb. Ghalib was one who saw it. His view encompassed the universe itself; as is evident from:

Hastee kay muth farayeb may ajayeeoo Asad
Aalam tamam halqa-e daam-e khayaal hai.

Be not deceived, O Asad, by the dazzle of creation
All existence is encircled, by the net of imagination.

The one distinctive aspect between man and the rest of the creation is his intellect. All things have good or bad effects depending on how they are viewed and employed. So also it is with the intellect. If intellect is endowed with a positive approach it leads to progress and achievement, but if enshrined in pessimism it destroys and destructs the edifice of life itself. The basis of intellect is thought and imagination. Out of which emerge all word and deed. It is this fact which Ghalib has so beautifully bejeweled in the verse above. A beautiful thought emanates from purity, and a vicious idea takes birth in the ugliness of contamination. Purity in its turn is inculcated by faith and belief, whereas impurity originates in doubt and deceit. It just goes to show what faith and belief Ghalib must have possessed. Ghalib tried to view the reality of Nature itself, but in its reflection saw his own image; since he said:

Sach kehtay hoe khud beene O', khud aara hun na kayuun hun ?
Baitha hai buth-e aaina seema meray aagay

True I am self observing, self admiring, why be it not so ?
Facing me is one whose forehead, like the mirror, is aglow.

Then Ghalib goes on to tackle the hidden mysteries of Nature and questions its underlying purpose. For he says:

Naqsh faryadee hai kis ke shokhi-e thareer ka
Kaghazi ha payrahan her paykarr-e tasweer ka

Whose dazzling work does the impression stricture ?
Of paper is the robe, of every figure in the picture.

The impression – the picture or creation, is questioning, crying out loud, for having been given the brilliance and the joy of being created; brought into existence and given the consciousness of it. Yet there is lament and pain of awareness because all is temporary and short-lived, just like the dress of paper of each figure face in the picture.
When he comes to behold beauty in Nature he questions its secrecy:

Jab woh jamal-e dil farooz, surat-e mehar-e neem rose
Aap he hoe nazara sooz, purdaey mein munh chuppaeye quon

When her radiance is heart enthrallingand appearance like the sun at noon.
Self-exposed and self-adoring, Why then in veil, she hides her bloom?

and then professes to explain its reason:

Dashna-e ghamza janistan, nawak-e naz bay panah
Taera hi ux-e rukh saahee, samnay taeray aayae quon

Like shooting arrow your demeanor, and dagger sharp your vanity.
Even your own faces shadow, in front of you why would it be?

This wonder, amazement and query then leads him to lament the fact -- the same conclusion as has been reached by philosophers like Plato, Pythagoras and others -- that man is fallen divinity. As is evident from his verse:

Na tha kutch to Khuda tha Kutch na hoota to Khuda hoota
Duboya mujh ko honay nay na hoota main to Kaya hoota?

When naught existed God existed, Had none there been, God would be.
My own existence lowered me. Would I not be, what would it be?

In the end I would like to leave the questioning mind with my question for Ghalib lovers to ponder, decipher accept or reject. For, if and when I meet Ghalib I will ask him as to why he did not write thus:

Na tha kutch to Khuda tha, Kutch na hoota to Khuda hoota
-Sujhaya- mujh ko honay nay, na hota main to Kaya hoota?

When naught existed God existed, Had none there been, God would be.
My very being, this made me see. Would I not be, what would it be?

For if I had not been brought forth I would no doubt have been part of the whole; but an insensitive, unconscious, ignorant part. My very being and individual existence gives me an identity of an entity and is responsible for making me aware of that fact.

AAH KO CHAHIYAY EIK UMR ASAR HONAY TAKK

Aah ko chahiyay eik umr asar honay takk
Koan jeeta hai teri zulf kay sir honay takk

A sigh needs an age, to show affect to the world.
Who can survive, till your cascade is uncurled.

(The concept of (aah) curse, sigh or silent complaint, is both religious and superstitious in the East. If someone suffers due to inexplicable reasons, it is said that s/he is suffering on account of another's curse or sigh. Here, Ghalib is saying that though even a curse shows its affect after a time, no one knows the length of time the beloved will take to groom her hair. May well be that he may perish and be consumed in the waiting.)

Daam har mauj mein hai halqa e saad kaam nahang
Dekhain qaya guzray hai quatray pay gohar hunay takk

Each desire takes a hundred effort, Before it can unfurl.
See, what all a drop has to go through, to become a valuable pearl.

(To get fulfillment of a desire one has to make devoted effort and a number of sacrifices, and has to patiently wait to see its achievement. Just like no one knows how difficult or tedious a process a drop of water has to pass through before it changes into a valuable pearl.)

Aashiqi sabr talab aur tamana baytaab
Dil ka kaya rung karoon khoon e jigar honay takk

Love endears patience, but desire is a restless flood.
What shade should I give to the heart, till my soul bleeds blood.

(Love matures slowly, but desire is difficult to control. What should one do to get peace of the heart while the process is being completed?

Eastern poetry has given both the heart and the soul (represented by the liver which is a much more deep rooted organ in the body) much prominence and importance in the human psyche. As, different from animals, man shows supremacy in both possessing and governing his emotions and feelings, and striving towards their fulfillment, in a conscious manner. The heart, though a physical organ, which primarily controls and pumps the flow of blood – the most vital fluid – has been epitomized as the body's jewel. But where does this blood come from, and what is its origin? It is the liver (inner being). So whereas the heart may hold the key of control; there would be nothing to control if the liver did not produce it in the first place. In Urdu poetry both heart and liver thus go together, hand in hand, with some sort of a love-hate relationship. Each envying, yet affirming the other's position. Something like the chicken and the egg story -- which came first and which holds sway? Overall however, the heart seems to get more attention from poets for it is the embodiment of delicacy and frailty. The heart is the seat of feelings and emotions, which at times shake the very edifice of human existence. The soul (inner being) on the other hand seems to be more enduring and more deep seated. It personifies the physique of man, and perhaps has more resilience. But if pain and sorrow are intense and unbearable, both heart and soul cry out in unison.)

Hum nay maana kay taghaful na karo gay lekin
Khaak hojayangay hum tum ko khabar honay takk

We admit you will not delay in the beckoning.
Yet, we would have turned to dust till your reckoning.

(Although the beloved may not delay and perhaps come quick on getting the news of the illness of the loved one, yet the news may take a long time to reach, and the poet may perish by then)

Partave khur say hai shabnam ko fana ki taleem
Mein bhi hoon eik inayat ki nazar honay takk

The dew learns to vanish, with the onset of sunlight.
I too wait, but just, for a single favour of sight.

(The water droplets of the overnight dew quickly evaporate with the coming of the heat of the sun, even in the shade. The beloved too gets consumed when the lover gives one glance, for which he waits all his life.)

Yak nazar beish nahin fursat e hasti ghafil
Garmi e bazam hai eik rakhs e sharrar honay takk

Not more than a wink is the freedom, to remain oblivious.
Only unto a dance of the spark, Is the warmth of the banquet, obvious.

(The carefree life is very short-lived and fleets by after a moment or two. For then, once again the worldly woes take hold, and remind one of the temporariness of bliss, and the emptiness of life itself.)

Gham e hasti ka Asad kis say ho juzz marg e illajj
Shama her rang mein jalti hai sehar honay takk

What can treat the torment of life, except death, O' Asad.
The candle keeps vigil till dawn, in all times, -- happy or sad.

(Life's strife only comes to end with the end of life itself. However, the process of living has to be borne and this life lived in all conditions and circumstance till then.)

AARZ E NIAZ E EISHQ KAY QABIL NAHIN RAHA

Aarz e niaz e eishq kay qabil nahin raha
Jis dil pay naaz tha mujhay who dil nahin raha

Did not remain capable of expressing love or emotion,
The heart I was so proud of has lost its touch for devotion.

(The poet was a lively person and perhaps full of life and happy all around. But his heart suffered so much pain and torture that it has become unconcerned and disenchanted, and does not feel even love any more.)

Jata hoon daag e hasrat e hasti liayay huayay
Hoon shama kushta dar khuray mehfil nahin raha.

I depart carrying the stain of unfulfilled existence.
Am but a burnt out candle, no sunlight to the audience.

(Life was spent in emptiness and desires remained unfulfilled and there is a feeling of dejection. It has been spent worthlessly providing no benefit to anyone.)

Marnay ki aay dil aur hi tarkeeb kar keh mein
Shahayan dast o Khanjar e qatil nahin raha.

Oh heart think of some other way To end life's strife.
I have not remained worthy of the killer's hand or knife.

(The feeling of self pity and worthlessness is so great that the poet feels he is even below the consideration and dignity of the killer and his knife.)

Her rooay shash jehat dar e aaina baaz hai
Yaan imtiaz e naaqis o kamil nahin raha.

Every worldly face is an open book Like a clear transparent glass.
Only I seem to have lost, the gauge of true worth and class.

(Simple verse but deep logic.)

Waa kar diayay hain shouq nay bund e naqaab e husan
Ghair az nigaha abb koi hayal nahin raha.

Desire's intensity has set apart, the drawn veils of beauty.
Except for the sight itself, now, there is no hindering entity.

(The desire is so strong that it has penetrated even the cover of the veil, and the true nature of the beauty has now become apparent. The vision is so near and clear, that except for the eye itself, there is nothing to hold back the view and perception.)

Go main raha, rahan e sitam, haaiy roozgar
Laykin teray khayal say ghafil nahin raha.

Though I stayed at the mercy of the pain of bread's earning.
But was surely not oblivious of your thoughts and yearning.

(Although the chores and needs of life kept the poet pinned down most of the time, leaving freedom for little else. Even then he did not forget the beloved and lived for loves fulfillment.)

Dil say, hava e kasht e wafa, mitt gayee, keh waan

Haasil siwaaye hasrat e haasil nahin raha

The heart lost its desire, to be faithful to admire.

What I gained from the pain, was just a longing for the gain.

(From the heart was erased the cultivation of faithfulness. There remained only pain and longing.)

Bay daad e eishq say nahin dar taa magar Asad

Jis dil pay naaz tha mujhay who dil nahin raha.

I do not fear, O Asad, the result of love's rejection.

The heart I was so proud of has lost its touch for devotion.

(The poet is not concerned for being rejected by the beloved any more, because the heart he was so dependent and proud of is no more the same.)

ASAD HUM WOOH JOONON JOOLAN GADAYA E BAY SIR O PAA HAIN

Asad hum wooh joonon joolan gadaya e bay sir o paa hain
Keh hai sir punja e mishgaan e ahoo pusht khaar apna

Asad we are those wayward beggars,
Shackled by the madness of desire;
Whose head is caught in the vices' of eyelashes,
And posterior is sunk in mire.

(The poet sees himself as those beggars who are completely lost in the shackles of love, because his mind is engrossed in the beauty of the beloved's eyelashes, and whose past is all a bundle of misgivings and full of failures. He has no idea where he is going or where he will end up.)

BAY EATEDALIOON SAY SUBUK SUB MAIN HUM HUAYAE

Bay eatedalioon say subuk sub main hum huayae
Jitnay ziada hoe gayae outnay he kum huayae

Through our reckless ways, no doubt, we became rather swift.
Yet, the smarter we did get, The more we went adrift.

(The poet is saying that though one achieves many worldly gains by becoming clever and shrewd, it is not essential one gets refined and progressive too.)

Pinhaan tha daam e sakht qareeb aashian kay
Ornay neh paayay thay keh griftaar hum huayae

There was a hidden trap, not far from the nest.
We hardly took to flight that we came under arrest.

(A simple and self explanatory verse.)

Hastee humari apni fana per daleel hai
Yaan takk mitay keh aap he apni qasam huayae

Our very existence is ample proof, of our own death to come.
We were trampled so much that, only in name, remained our total sum.

(Life is proof enough that death will come. The world and its ways destroyed the poet so much that nothing worth the name remained.)

Sakhti kashan e eishq ki puchay hai kaya khabar
Who loug rafta rafta sarapa alam huayae

O' what news do you ask, of love's downtrodden.
They were all steadily lost, and alas were forgotten.

(Quite a self explanatory verse.)

Tayree wafa say kaya hoe talafee keh dehar main
Teray siva bhee hum pay bohat say sitam huayae

Your faithfulness is not enough to wash off the pains that were hurled.
For, besides you, others too gave us much hardship in this world.

(Simple verse.)

Likhtay rahay junoon ki hikayaat e khoon chikan
Harchand iss main haath humaray qalam huayae

Kept writing the blood-stained tales, of madness, and it woe.
For even though our hands were severed in doing so.

(The poet devotedly kept engaged in writing his sad story. The tale was so intense that his hands started to bleed.)

Allah ree taree tundiaye khoo jis kay baym say
Ajza e nala dil main meray riziq e hum huayae

O' God the might of your rage and your demeanor too, my dear.
The ingredients of complaint hid in my heart out, of fear.

(For fear of the rage and temper of the beloved, the poet could not even bring himself to register a complaint.)

Ahlay havis ki fatah hai tark e nabard e eishq
Joe pawoon uth gaaye wohee ounkay alam huayae

Shunning the quarrel of love, is victory for the yearning soul.
They put in good effort, in the way of the lofty goal.

(In the long run, those who harness the uncontrolled ego are bound to reach the goal and establish their superiority.)

Naalay addam main chund humaray supurd thay
Joe waan neh khinch sakay so wooh yaan aakay dum huayae

Some wailing and complaints, were in our share since oblivion.
They came out loud, here and now, those we could not utter then.

(The poet says that man was destined to suffer and complain from the time of his inception. The complaints he did not make before, are bound to be uttered sooner or later.)

Chooree Asad neh hum nay gadaee main dil lagee.
Sael huayae toe ashiqq e eahel e karam huayae

Even in beggary O' Asad we did not lose our taste.
For although asking for alms, admired the giver's grace.

Ghalib says though he is a beggar and lives on alms yet he still appreciates and admires the beauty of the giver.)

BAZICHA E ATFAAL HAI DUNIYA MERAY AAGAY

Bazicha-e atfaal hai duniya meray aagay
Hoota hai shab o rose tamasha meray aagay

Like child's play Is this world, in front of me.
There is enacted, Night and day, a scene to be.

(The poet says he fathoms much and is very aware of things around. The world and its happenings seem like child's play. The scene he sees all around is quite like that of a drama where every man acts out his role and moves on. The poem, if read carefully, seems to be a combination of being an ode to man and at the same time a query based on human doubts and misgivings as to what in reality is his nature and purpose.)

Eaik khaiyal hai aurang-e Suleman meray nazdeek
Eaik baat hai eayjaaz-e Massiha meray aagay

The throne of solomon is but a toy before me.
The miracle of the messiah is but a ploy before me.

(Even the most valuable of things of this world are like toys. The poet is so far ahead in his thinking that even the miracles performed by messiah (Jesus) seem to be just stories and myths.)

Juzz naam nahin surat-e aalam mujhay manzoor
Juzz weyham nahin haste-e ashiya meray aagay

Except in name, the condition of the world is not acceptable to me.
The existence of things is nothing, but a figment of my imagery.

(The world as it exists is not truly how it should be. Most things are not real but a figment of ones imagination).

Hoota hai nehaan gard mein sehrah meray hootay
Ghista hai jabeen khaak pay dariya meray aagay

Seeks refuge in the dust, the desert, due to my presence.
Rubs its forehead on the sand, The river, in my reverence.

(Here the poet has raised the level of man to such a height that even natural phenomena respect and revere him.)

Muth pooch keh kaya haal hai mera teray pechay
Tou deikh keh kaya rang hai tera meray aagay

Oh! do not ask how I fare in your absence.
Just see how you bloom, when in my presence.

(This is typical of Ghalib's reasoning and logic as he always takes an oblique angle to see things and reasons for them in his own unique way.)

Such khetay ho khud bein o khud ara hoon
na kayuun hoon?
Beitha hai buth-e aaina seema meray aagay

True, I am self observing, self admiring, Why be it not so?
Facing me is one whose forehead, Like a mirror, is aglow.

(The beauty and depth of this verse is admirable and shows the flight of the poet's thoughts that put him face to face with the Creator Himself. It is an extremely beautiful way of asking if we are made in the image of God or vice versa ?)

Phir daekhiay andaaz-e gul afshani-e guftaar
Rakh dae kooei paimana-e saiba meray aagay

Then see me speak a tongue so full, of flowery prose;
let some one place before me wine, Red, like a radiant rose.

(This is quite self explanatory).

Nafrat ka guman guzray hai mein rashk say guzzra
Kayuun kar kahoon low naam na ounka meray aagay

It seems with distaste, though I passed by full -aflame.
How , should I say, "Don't remind me of her name."

(The shyness of the East and its tradition of respect made the poet pass by the lady love with his eyes lowered, which gave the wrong impression. It is even difficult for him to tell others not to remind him of her, for it evokes pain of longing in his heart).

Eemaan mujahy rookay hay tou kheenchay hai mujahy kuffr
Kaba meray pichay hai kalisaa meray aagay

Faith pulls me to itself, yet sin drags by exciting.
Kabah from behind me restraining, the Chapel in front, enticing.

(This is an exemplary verse, showing the conflict of human nature. The tussle of good and evil are clearly pointed out here, and the verse shows every man's dilemma.)

Aashiq hoon pah mashooq farabee hai mera kaam
Majnoon ko bura kahtee hai duniya meray aagay

I am a lover, but beloved deception is my taste.
The devoted Majnoon is ridiculed, in front of my face.

(The poet says that he is a naughty lover for he likes to tease the beloved. The purity of devotion of Majnoon, the famous lover of Laila, is embarrassed by the poet's behaviour).

Khush hotay hain par vasal mein yoon marr naheen jataay
Aayee shab-e hijraan ke tamanna meray aagay

One is overjoyed yet, none dies as such in love's fulfillment and delight.
There came before me face to face, the wish of the separation's night.

(The intricate logic is that, usually everyone is very pleased on the honey moon's night and hardly any one dies out of delight. The poet however, died of happiness on the night of fulfillment, and he explains his death as the attainment of the wish of the 'night of separation'; --- which was to keep the lovers apart).

Hai mawjzan eik qulzum-e khoon, kash yehee ho
Aata hai abhee daekheay kaya kaya meray aagay

There is a tumultuous sea of blood; Lord! may that be just it. -- Though,
Remains to be seen, what else before me, is yet to come and go.

(The present condition of the poet's love is in itself a torturous route, like a sea of blood. Yet what else lies ahead remains to be seen).

Go haath ko jumbish naheen aankhoon mein to dum hai
Rahe nay doo abhi saghaar O meena meray aagay

Though the hand cannot move, the eye still can choose.
Let there be wine and drink before me, if only for excuse.

(Quite self explanatory).

Hum pesha o hum mashroob o hum raaz hai mera
Ghalib ko bura kayun, kahoo acha meray aagay

My colleague, sharer of the cup and secret, is he.
Call Ghalib not names, praise him, in front of me.

(Simple and self explanatory verse.)

BUS KEH DUSHWAR HAI HER KAAM KA AASAAN HOONA

Bus keh dushwar hai her kaam ka aasaan hoona
Aadmi ko bhi maiyasar naheen insaan hoona

Alas! Difficult is the way for any task to accomplish, with ease.
For man too, is not certain to become human,
were he even so to wish, or please.

(The poet is lamenting the fact that it is not easy to accomplish any task in this world, so much so that even if man wishes to become refined and humane, it is not easy at all.)

Girya chahay hai kharabee maray kashanay ke
Dar o diwar say tapkay hai biabaan hoona

The sad state of my abode wants to cry out and weep.
Utter neglect, from its walls and doors, ooze forth and seep.

(Relatively simple verse.)

Waay divangee e shouq, keh her dum mujh ko
Aap jana udhar, aur aap he parayshaan hoona

O! the madness of desire, that every time,
Myself I go there, and get astonished once I am there.

(In the intensity of desire the poet goes to the beloved's house, but when he reaches there he is stupefied and surprised at his own act.)

Jalva azbaskay taqaza e nigha karta hai
Johar e aayeena bhi chahay hai mishgaan hoona

As glory wherefore, reminds the eye, to look and see;
The mirror's essence, itself wants, to become the reflected entity.

(This is a very philosophical verse and should be seen in much broader light. The poet says a beautiful sight compels the viewer to see and admire it, and perhaps the image or man aspires to merge into the Creator itself- i.e. God.)

Ishrat e qatalgah e ehailay tamana mutt pooch
Eid e nazara hai, shamsheer ka urian hoona

Do not ask the bliss of the alter, of the desirer's deep faith.
Joy unlimited is, the sight of the sword, being drawn, from its sheath.

(The very alter of sacrifice, the place where the desire of the devoted is going to be shattered, itself starts celebrating, the moment it sees the sword coming out of the sheath in the murderer's hand. For then it knows the victim is being brought for slaughter.)

Lay gayay khaak main hum dagh e tamana e nishat
Tou hoe aur aap basadd rang e gulistan hoona

We took the stain of yearning of the desire, right to the grave.
Just to be with yourself, and to keep a hundred garden enslave.

(The poet says he died in waiting for the fulfilment of his simple desire to be with the lady love. For, to get that desire is like having a hundred gardens in one's palm.)

Ishrat e para e dil zakhm e tamana khana
Lazat e reesh e jigar, araq e namakdan hoona

The satisfaction for a mercurial heart is to devour the wound of desire;
Real taste of the imbedded pain, is in essence at the pit of the pyre.

(The intricacy of the verse is in its metaphors where the poet says that the way to get some solace for the heart is keep nagging at itself and its desires, and the soul gets purified after being embroiled in the fire of tragedy.)

Kee meray qatal kay baad ous nay jafa say toubah
Haye ous zood pashemaan ka pashemaan hoona

After killing me she took the oath of piety, and a vow not to snare.
Oh! What gallantry by the gallantless, to feel and show such care.

(A rather simple verse)

Haif iss chaar girah kapray ki qismat Ghalib
Jis ke qismat main hoe aashiq ka garibaan hoona

Alas! Ghalib, The luck of that cloth's small tatter,
Whose destiny it is to be the lover's collar.

(The poet is pitying the lover's collar. It is that part of the garment which is usually ruffled, unattended and open. It also symbolises the portion of the dress that is easily gripped when accusing and assaulting.)

..TKASHAY DAVA NA HOUA

Dard minatkashay dava na houa
Mein na achha houa bura na houa

The pain did not have to beg the remedy for cure;
That I did not get well, was not bad, for sure.

(The self pride of the poet is praising his endurance and, that he did not have to stoop low and plead the medicine for relief. That the important thing is his self respect was preserved, it does not really matter that he did not get well or cured.)

Jama kartay hoe qayoon raqiboon ko
Eik tamasha houa gila na houa

You gather all the rivals for what plaint?
Seems more like a jest than a complaint.

(A complaint, specially to one near and dear, is usually made quietly. So if the beloved insists on gathering all the rivals to register it, it seems more of a fanfare than serious talk).

Hum kanhan qismet aazmanay jayain
Tou bhi jub khanjar aazma na houa

Where should we go to seek award?
When even you are not, willing to try the sword.

(The poet feels so rejected that the beloved does not even tease and torture. There is no place else to go.)

Kitnay shereen hain teray lub kay raqeeb
Galian kha kay bay maza na houa

How sweet are your tongue's watchful admirers.
Even after abuses they do not lose their desires.

(Raqeeb are rivals and admirers who act here as guards. Even when the lover rebukes and abuses them away they still remain devoted and steadfast and do not leave.)

Hai khabar garm oun kay aanay ki
Aaj he ghar mein bouria na houa

It is hot news that they will be coming.
Just today the house has no provision or bedding.

(Simple verse.)

Kaya who Namrood ki khudai thee
Bundagi mein mara bahala na houa

What was the good of Nimrod's godness.
He died in bondage, achieving no goodness.

(Nimrod was a pharaoh who was famous for his pomp and show. Even he died like a human, nothing could help him. What a pity.)

Jan dee, dee houi ousi ki thee
Haqq toe yeh hai kay haqq ada na houa

Gave life, was given it by Him alone.
Truth is no justice by me, was done.

(The poet says that he gave up his life. In the end it was from Him (God). The fact is he did not fulfill his duties in this world, for he did nothing worthwhile during his life time.)

Zakham gar dub gaya lahoo na thama
Kam gar rukgaya rava na houa

Though the wound receded, the bleeding has not ceased.
The work if stopped, leaves no one really pleased.

(The wound of the heart has been filled up but the bleeding did not stop. This half action has neither made him well not put him to death.)

Rehzani hai keh dilsitani hai
Lay kay dil dilsitaan ravana houa

Is it highway man-ship or winning of the heart?
Upon snatching the heart, the lover did quickly depart.

(The poets heart was snatched away violently. He feels this is 'day light robbery'.)

Kutch toe parhheay keh loog kehtay hain
Aaj Ghalib gazalsara na houa

Recite something for people say;
Ghalib seems to have nothing today.

(Simple verse.)

DHAMKI MAIN MAR GAYA JOE NEH BAB E NABARD THA

Dhamki main mar gaya joe neh bab e nabard tha
Eishq e nabard paishaye talabgar mard tha

Died in just a threat, in the war, who showed no valour or class.
The war of love was a profession, of man's manliness – alas!

(The poet says that love is a game of manliness and not for the faint of heart, who would turn away from it on receiving a few rebukes from the beloved or tortures on the way of it.)

Tha zindigi main marg ka khatka laga hua
Urhnay say paishtar bhi mera rang zrd tha

During life I could feel the fear of ultimate loss of breath,
Even before the loss of colour my face was pale as death.

(Simple verse)

Taleef e nushkha hai wafa kar raha tha main
Majmooaya e khail abhi fard fard tha

Was compiling the formula of faithfulness with all of my wit.
The complete volume of thought, however, was yet only bit upon bit.

(The poet says he is trying to write the rules of faithfulness for the lovers, and is using all his intellect to come up with a viable formula, however, the more he tries he cannot come up with a fool proof prescription.)

Dil ta jigar keh sahil e daryae khoon hai abb
Is rehguzar main jalvae gul aagay gard tha

The heart and soul are shores of flowing blood, from here to there.
On this road, the beauty of the rose was a pathway of sand, as it were.

Jaati hai koi kashmakesh undvehe ishq ki
Dil bhi agar gaya toe whahee dil ka dard tha

Does the torture of the ailing heart ever go away?
Itself, the heart may be lost, the pain is there to stay.

Ehabab chara sazaeeay wahshat neh kar sakay
Zindaan main bhi, khayal biabaan navard tha

Companions could not console and make the tumultuous heart any mild.
Even though locked up in prison, the thoughts wandered in the wild.

Yeh laash e bay kafan Asad khasta jaan ke hai
Haq magfirat karay! Ajab aazad mard tha

This corpse unenshrouded Is of asad Ullah the fragile.
May the Lord forgive him, with... he however, had a very brave profile,

DIAYAM PARA HUA TERAY DAR PAR NAHIN HOON MEIN

Diayam para hua teray dar par nahin hoon main
Khak ayasee zindigi pay keh pathar nahin hoon main

Endlessly lying by your door, -- Is not I am.
Dust beget such life, for a stone, -- Is not I am.

(The poet says he is tired of waiting for the beloved to come out and that he will not stay at the door for ever. He says such life be cursed, and that he is not a stone that will continue to lie there.)

Kayuun gardish e madaam say ghabra neh jaayay dil
Insan hoon piyala o saghar naheen hoon main

Why should the heart not tire, of the endless rotation?
Human am I, a cup or wine flask, -- Is not I am.

(He says that he is fed up of the endless passing of the days and nights. He feels his heart is tired of constant rotation and is not a wine cup or decanter, which keeps moving from person to person without complaining.)

Yaa rab zamana mujh koo mita ta hai kis liyay
Lohaay jehan pay harafay mukaraar mahin hoon mein

Oh! Lord, why does the world try to efface me?
On the earth's metal, the word - repeat, -- Is not I am.

(Here he says that he will not return to the world again and again, so why are people bent upon getting rid of him.)

Hadd chahiyay saza main uqoobat kay wastay
Aakhir gunahgar hoon kafir nahin hoon mein

There should be restraint in punishment for reformation to set in.
A sinner am I, after all, a heretic, -- Is not I am.

(Simple verse. Does not need any explanation.)

Kis wastay aziz nahin jantay mujhay
Lal O Zumurod O Zar O Ghohar nahin hoon mein

Why am I not considered to be valuable?
Ruby, pearl, wealth or jewel, -- Is not I am.

(The poet stresses the point that he is human. Why should man not be considered more valuable than jewels and be treated such?)

Rakhtay ho tum qadam mayree ankhoon say qayoon daraegh
Rutbay mein mehar O mah say kamtar naheen hoon mein.

Why from my view do you stealthily move?
In status, below the sun and moon, -- Is not I am.

(Once again the poet goes to stress the superiority of humans, who should be considered above and higher in station than even the sun or moon, and as to why should people ignore and avoid him.)

Kartay ho mujh ko mana qadam boos kis liay
Kaya aasman kay bhee barabarr naheen hoon mein

Why do you forbid me to touch your feet?
Is it that, even as the high sky, -- Is not I am.

(Now here the poet takes man to loftier heights than even the sky which touches the feet of the earth. He wonders why he is not even allowed to be of service to humanity.)

Ghalib wazeefa khowar ho doo shah koo dua
Wooh dinn gayay joo khatay thae naukar nahin hoon main

You live on pension, Ghalib. Ask blessings for the King.
Gone are the days when you said, a servant, -- Is not I am.

(Ghalib was a very upright and a proud man. But, since he started getting a stipend from the court he had to sing the ruler's praise and compromise his self pride. It is this fact he is lamenting in the verse.)

DIL HE TO HAI NA SANG O KISHIST

Dil he too hai na sang o kishisht dard say bhaar na aaye qayoon
Rooayan gay hum hazar bar koi haumay sataye qayoon.

It's but a heart, stone nor brick, with pain why would it not over-flow.
We will weep a thousand times, why should someone tease us so?

(If some one teases, the heart, which is not made of stone, is bound to get hurt.)

Dayar nahin haram nahin dar nahin aastaan nahin
Baithay hain rahguzar pay hum ghair humain uthaye qayoon

Not a temple or house of God. no one's door or a saint's abode.
By the wayside we do sit, pray why! should then, strangers goad?

(Here the poet says he is not disturbing any one, nor is he sitting at some one's property. He is merely sitting at the cross roads of life. Why should any passerby disturb or trouble him.)

Jub wooh jamal-e dil farooz surat-e mehare neemrooz
Aap he hoo nazara sooz parday main munh chupayae qayoon

When her radiance is heart enthralling, and appearance, like the sun at noon;
Self-exposed and self-adoring, why then in veil, she hides her bloom?

(In a broader sense the poet is admiring and questioning Nature itself. Note the philosophical probe and enquiry at the end of it.)

Dashna-e ghamza jaanistan nawak-e naaz baypanah
Taira he ux-e rukh sahee samnay taire aaye qayoon

Like shooting arrow your demeanor, and dagger sharp your vanity;
Even your own faces shadow, in front of you why would it be?

(In this verse the poet gives explanation of the reason for the hiding of the deity of the previous verse. He says it is difficult for any one or any thing to face such a being who is so full of agility, grace, conceit and valor. Note that even its own shadow can not bear to face it for fear of being trampled and destroyed.)

Qaid-e hayat O band-e gham asal main doono aik hain
Mauth say phalay aadmi gham say nijaat payae qayoon

The prison of life and woeful human suffering, Are one and the same thing.
Why then, before death should man, Be free of sorrow and the pain?

(To go through this life is a constant battle and struggle that has to be endured. There is no escape from it till death.)

Husan aur ous pay husan-e zan rah gaie boo alhavis ki sharm
Upany pay eitaymaad hoo to ghair ko aazmaye qayoon

Beauty, and then topped with vanity, only remains an envier's shame.
(This is pun at its best)
If one has the self confidence, then why test another's frame?

(The beloved is so beautiful and also conceited, yet is full of jealousy. There must be some insecurity. For, if one is self confident then why should he/she worry about what others have.)

Wan who ghuroor O Uzz O naaz yan yeh hijab e paas e waza
Rah mein hum milayan kahaan, bazam mein wooh bulaye qayoon

There the pride, vanity, and conceit, here, the shyness, and tradition of the East.
On the way we cannot meet, and why would she call us to her feast?

(Self contained.)

Haan who nahin khuda parast jaayoo who bewafa sahee
Jis ko ho deen O dil azeea yus ki gali mein jayae qayoon

Admitted she's not God fearing; Yes, she may be unfaithful -- So!
Who holds dear her heart and faith; To her lane then, why should one go?

(The poet knows fully well that the beloved is not God fearing, and consequently may be unfaithful too. This is all very well. For, if she was faithful and held her heart very dear it would be futile to try and woo her.)

Ghalib e khasta kay baghair kon say kaam bund hain
Royiyae zaar zaar qaya kijiyae hai hai qayoon

Without old tattered Ghalib, what work cannot proceed?
Why then weep incessantly, and cry one's heart out to bleed?

(Simple, self explanatory)

DIL SAY TAREE NIGHAH JIGAR TAK UTAR GAIYEE

Dil say taree nigah jigar tak utar gaiyee
Doonoon ko eik adda mein razamand kar gaiyee

Your look penetrated, from the heart to the soul.
Winning over both of them, in a single roll.

(The intensity of the look was so strong and piercing, and that the impact of the stab so heavy, that not only did the heart lose a beat but the pain was felt deep down in the soul. It shattered both the defenses in a single blow. Reflect upon the impact the one Beatrice would have had on Dante, or the other Beatrice would had on David, father of king Solomon.)

Shaqq ho gaya hai seena khusha lazat e firaaq
Takleef purda dareay zakaham e jigar gaiyee

The chest has parted, bravo! O' delight of separation -- see.
The pain, of keeping hidden the inner wound, will no longer be.

(The poet is sarcastically praising his own intensity of desire which has opened up his chest, and the internal wounds are now exposed for everyone to see. There remains no reason or pull of tradition and culture to keep them under cover.)

Who bada e shabana ki sarmastian kahaan
Uthiaye bus abkay lazat e khaab e sehar gaiyee

Where are the light-hearted moods of the drunken night?
Get up, for the ecstasy of morning dreams, has taken flight.

(Self explanatory verse.)

Urtee phiray hai khaak meri kooyay yar mein
Baray ab aay hava, hawiss e bal o par gaiyee

My ashes keep floating in the lover's lane.
Alas! for now, gone is the greed of gain.

(The greed to gain the closeness of the beloved was the lover's desire all his life. Now that life has ended and he has been cremated, perhaps the ashes have found their way to the beloved's lane and there is no more need for that desire.)

Dekhoo to dilfarabeay andaz e naqsh o paa
Mauj e kharam e yar bhi kaya gul katar gaiyee

See the heart throbbing beauty of her hand and feet.
The seductive walk of my love, cut even the flowers all so neat.

(The poet is praising the graceful and charming ways of the beloved. As pe him, her walk is so sharp and seductive that it can even cut the delicate flowers quite neatly.)

Her booalhavis nay husanparasti shaar ke
Ab aabroo e shewa e ahle nazar gaiyee

Every envier donned ways of beauty admiration.
Gone is the dignity of the elitist's way of expression.

(The poet says that when every Tom, Dick and Harry starts to admire and stare at the beauty, it hurts its dignity. The subtle ways of the lovers of the east, who only gave dignified glances, have lost their value.)

Nazaray nay bhi kaam kiya waan naqaab ka
Mustee say her nigah teray rukh par bikhar gaiyee

The scene itself acted there, as a veil of chaste.
Every look spread on your face, as if in a drunken state.

(The view was so magnificent that the sight itself acted as a protective veil. The viewer was overwhelmed by the beauty and got in a state of stupor and could only see the face in a drunken state –It was blurred and not clear, as if from behind a veil.)

Fardawari ka tafriqa yakbar mit gaya
Kul tum gayay keh hum pay qaimat guzar gaiyee

The sense of duality, for once was wiped out.
You departed yesterday, and we bore hell's bout.

(This verse is typical of Ghalib's pun and metaphor. He is describing the similarity of feelings of the lover and beloved at the moment of parting. Both seem to suffer with equal intensity, one at the parting and the other at departing.)

Mara zamanay nay Asadullah Khan tumhain
Who walwalay khaan who jawani kidhar gaiyee

You were destroyed by the world, O' Asadullah Khan.
Where went the lively ambitions? And the youth too is all now gone.

(The poet is expressing dejection at having tried so hard to do good for the world and humanity at large, yet not being acclaimed by any one for it, and that now all desire and ambition is lost.)

FARIGH MUJHAY NEH JAAN KEH MANIND E SUBH O MEHR

Farigh mujhay neh jaan keh manind e subh o mehr
Hai daagh e ishq zeenat e jaib e kafan hanooz

Do not consider me spotless and free, for like the morning's sun, so proud,
The stain of love ever shines, on the pocket of my shroud.

(The poet says that his life has not been all serene and peaceful since he fell in love. It is like the morning sun as it stands out in the clear sky and seems a stain on the white coffin cloth.)

Hai naaz e muflisan zar azdast rafta par
Houn gul faroosh e shokhi e dagh e kohan hanooz

A Poor man is still proud of his wealth, spent thriftily by.
I keep recounting the flowery dazzle of the old stain of the sty.

(A person who has been hit with poverty keeps recounting the times of his wealthy days, and his plundered wealth. So the poet keeps remembering his shiny wound that had been inflicted by his beloved.)

Maikhana e jigar main yahaan khaak bhi naheen
Khamiaza khinchaay hai buth e baydaadfun hanooz

In the tavern of the heart, even a drop of blood does not remain.
Yet the relentless beloved, squeezes me in the torturer's frame.

(The poet says that he does not even have a drop of blood in his body yet the beloved is bent upon torturing and squeezing him.)

GAYEE WHO BATH KE HOE GUFTOGOO TOE KYUNKAR HOE

Gayee woh bath keh hoe guftogoo toe kyunkar hoe
kahay say kutch na hua phir kahoo, toe kyunkar hoe

Its past the stage of 'break the ice', then, --How should it be?
Naught came forth with talk, so say now, --How should it be?

(The poet is saying that it is past the stage where one thinks as to how to initiate conversation. Now that even conversation does not bring about the desired results so what should be done?)

Hamaray zehan mein iss fikar ka hai naam -- visal
keh gar na hoe toe kahan jaayian, ho, toe kyunkar hoe.

In our mind this worry is called -- fulfillment.
For if happens not, where should one go?
For it to happen, -- How should it be?

(He is thinking about the fulfillment of his heart's desire. The question is as to where should one go to find peace when the wish is not fulfilled, and the next worry is what is the way to find it?)

Adab hai, aur yehei kashmakash too kaya kijiaye
Hayya hai aur yehei goomaggo, toe kyunkar hoe

There is regard yet also this conflict, what is to be done?
For shyness restrains and desire excites, --what could it be?

(From the poet's side the respect for traditions confounds him. On the beloved's side it is shyness and the shame. How then would fulfillment be achieved?)

Tum he kahoo keh guzara sanam parastoon ka
buthoon ke hoe agar aysei he khoo, toe kyunkar hoe

You Say yourself , if the idols have such bloated ego,
Then for their worshipers, ease in life, --How would it be?

(If the idols that the idolaters worship, have such inflated egos that they are not even ready to listen, then where else will the worshipers go to seek peace?)

Ulhajtay hoe tum agar dekhtay hoe aaiyana
Joe tum say sheher mein houn eik doe, toe kyunkar hoe.

When you see the mirror, you irritate.
If in the city there are a few like you, --How would it be?

(The beloved is so temperamental that seeing her own face in the mirror irritates her. If there be a few others with the same attitude life would become hell.)

Jisay naseeb hoe rose-e sihah mera saa
voh shaksh dinn na kahay rath ko, toe kyunkar hoe

One who is fated with dark days like me,
If he does not call night to be day, --Why should it be?

(The poet says his fate is dark like a night and so what is wrong if he sees the night to be day? He can't see the difference anyway.)

Hamain phir un say omeed aur onhain hamari qadar
Hamari baath he puchain na voh, toe kyunkar hoe

For us to pin hope on them and they to give us regard,
When they don't even listen to us, --How would it be?

(What hope is there when the beloved does not even enquire about the lover. How would there be any expectation of caring for each other?)

Ghalat na tha humaiyan khat pur gumaan tasalii ka
Na manay deeda o deedaar, toe kyunkar hoe

Our suspicion, that the letter was but a consolation, was not wrong.
Being face to face she doesn't agree, --Then how should it be?

(The poet's feeling that the letter sent by the beloved was just a consolation, turned out to be right. For he knew that, if she did not agree in face to face talk how could she be expected to give in otherwise?)

Battaoo iss mezhaa ko dekh kar hoe mujh ko qaraar
Yeh neish ho rag-e jaan mein faroe, toe kyunkar hoe

Say, on seeing these eye-lashes can I get peace?
They, that are embedded in my jugular vein, --How would it be?

(The poet says that these eyelashes which are so penetrating and hurtful can hardly give him any comfort. Yet they are most enchanting yet so deeply pinching.)

Mujhay junoon nahin Ghalib, valay baqool huzoor
Firaaq-e yaar mein taskeen hoe, toe kyunkar hoe

I am not demented Ghalib, but as you say,
In the quest of love -- peace, --How could it be?

(The poet says that he is not mad. Yet, even as the beloved confirms herself, it is difficult to get peace in love.)

GAR KHAMOOSHI SY FAIDA AKHFAE HAAL HAI

Gar khamooshi say faida akhfae haal hai
Khush hoon keh mayree baat samajhna mohal hai

If silence is beneficial for the hidden present state,
Pleased I am that, my talk is difficult to contemplate.

(Ghalib says that it is good no one understands his talk, as it is in the interest of things to be kept under cover at the moment.)

Kis ko sunayoon hasrat e izhar ka gila
Dil fard jama o kharch zaban haiyay lal hai

Who can I tell? the unexpressed desire of love's tale.
Head lost in give and take, the tongue red and pale.

(Ghalib says it is really difficult to find someone in who one can confide. The head is lost in the uncertainty of decision as to who to tell , yet the tongue is tired of repetitions of the sorrowful tale.)

Kis purday main hai aaina pardaaz ayae khuda
Rehmat, keh uzar khowa e lub bay sawal hai

Under what cover , O' God, is the mirror gazing one.
Please forgive, that even the excuse making tongue is gone.

(The poet is waiting for his self adoring beloved to come out of the parlor. He is asking for forgiveness for his much demanding tongue, which has now fallen silent.)

Hai Hai khuda na khawasta wooh aur dushamani
Aaye shouq e munfail yeh tujahay kaya khaiyal hai

Oh no! God may forbid, she and enmity?
Oh shameful desire. What kind of thought this be?

(The poet says that his beloved is beyond being envious of any, and he is reprimanding himself for even getting such doubtful thoughts about her.)

Wahshat pay maree arsa e afaaq thang tha
Darya zameen ko arqq e infaal hai

For my frustration the heaven's time length,
was short and little, somehow.
The sea is but the sweat of embarrassment, on the earth's brow.

(Ghalib says that for his uncontrolled feelings even the entire heaven's duration was not enough. He describes the water of seas of the world is in reality the sweat of the earth's frustration about its unfulfilled efforts.)

Hasti kay mutt faraib main aajaiou Asad
Alam tamam halqa e dam e khayal hai

Be not deceived O' Asad, by the dazzle of creation.
All existence is encircled, by the net of imagination.

(Asad { an earlier pseudonym of Ghalib} says that man should not get enticed by the glamour of the world, as all this but a figment of one's imagination. Whose who can say?

GHAM KHANAY MEIN BODAA DIL E NAKAM, BOHAT HAI

Gham khanay main bodaa dil e nakam, bohat hai
Yeh ranj keh kum hai mai e gulfam, bohat hai

To bear misery, this heart of mine, is not strong at all.
That, colorful wine is short, Is enough to make it bawl.

(The verse just goes to show the extreme sensitivity and emotional nature of the poet, who gets disturbed and upset due to ever such small causes.)

Kehtay huaye saqi say haya aati hai warna
Hai yoon keh mujhay durdd tahay jaam bohat hai

Feel embarrassed to tell the saqi – but yet.
I know there is much residue, at the base of my goblet.

(The tradition and culture of the East keeps the poet from complaining and even mentioning to the saqi (usually personified by a hostess in a drink parlor – who in Urdu poetry is a very revered and beloved person.), that there is much residue at the base of the cup. However, whatever the saqi serves is usually taken with a smile and without complaint, with a pinch of salt, so to say. It is considered that it is the saqi's drink which is the source of life and eternal peace and bliss, as much as, that the saqi at times connotes the deity itself, who gives the taste of the drink of life.)

Nay teer Kaman main hai neh sayaad kameen main
Goshay main qafas kay mujhay aaram bohat hai.

Neither is the arrow in the bow , nor the hunter on the mount.
In the corner of the prison, i am at peace on all count.

(There is no danger of getting shot down. For once in the cage there is no fear of being hunted down.)

Kaya zuhood ko manoon keh neh hoe garchay rayaee
Padash e amal ki tamma, khaam bohat hai.

Why piety should I acclaim? it may well conquer the ego;
To gain is the aim of every act, however pious it be, though.

(A pious person seems to have over come this world's desires and fears, because he claims to fear none other than God. But he too, however pious he may be, is looking forward to a reward in the next life, and it is perhaps that illusion which makes him worship much and give up this world for the benefits of the next.)

Hain ehal e khirad kis rawish e khaas peh nazaan
Pabastigee e rasam o rreh , aam bohat hai

On what special account, do men of wisdom feel so proud.
The tradition of 'touching-feet' is still rampant, all about.

(Even in most perfect systems merit alone cannot succeed. Some form of pleasing the boss always exists in society. For, it's not what you are but who you know that takes you far -- at least in the worldly ways)

Zamzam hee peh choroo, mujhay kaya towfay haram say
Aloodah bay mai , jama e ehram bohat hai.

Leave me at the water-well, what need I, to go the rounds.
In stains, though not of wine, my ritual robe abounds.

(Zam zam is the spring of water in the Kaba, at Mecca. There pilgrims throng to quench their thirst, perform ablution and cleanse them-

selves when circumambulating the Kaba.
Here the poet says it is better for him to remain at the Zam Zam for he is not yet clean to perform the rounds of Kaba, as his garment, meaning his self, is stained with enough sin and much remorse.)

Khoon hoe kay jigar aankh say tapka naheen, ay marg!
Rehnay doe mujhay yaan , abhi kaam bohat hai

Oh! Malady, my soul has not dropped as a tear of blood, just yet.
Let me still be here for I have, lots to do and much regret.

(He is addressing his own illness and says there is still more room for pain, because though he sheds tears they are still just of water and do not show the intensity of blood. So he feels there is still lot to bear and withstand in order to pay for all his ills.)

Hooga koi ayesa bhee keh Ghalib ko neh janay
Shaiyr toe woh acha hai peh budnam bohat hai

Would there be such a one, who does not know Ghalib's name.
A good poet he sure is, but has acquired much ill-fame.

(Self explanatory verse.)

GHUNCHA E NASHAGUFTA KO

Ghuncha e nashagufta ko dour say mautt dikha keh youn
Bosay ko poochata hoon main munh say mujhay bataa keh youn

Do not show the budding bouquet from far away, ... just like so.
I ask about a kiss, show me with your lips, ... just like so.

(The poet is comparing the beloved's lips to a bouquet of budding flowers. He says they are not for showing from a distance but are worthy of being kissed.)

Purshish e tarz e dilbaree kijiay kaya keh bin kahay
Ous kay her aik isharay say niklay hai yeh aada keh youn

What need ask, how to please the lady-love? for without saying,
Her every hint and sign does show, as if to say,... just like so.

(Simple verse and does not need further elaboration.)

Raat kay waqt mai piay saath raqeeb ko liay
Aaye wo yaan khuda karay, pur na karay khuda keh youn

Having had a drink at night and in the rival's company,
May lord she come here, but no lord, not,... just like so.

(The poet hopes that the beloved comes to visit him after having had a drink and accompanied with his rival, but then he hopes that it is not so, i.e. she should come without the rival.)

Ghair say raat kaya bani, yeh jo kaha toe daikheayay
Samnay aan baithna aur yeh daikhna keh youn

This I asked, how did it go with the stranger, last night?
She came to sit face to face and gazed at me, as if to say,... just like so.

(When the poet asked about the loves venture with the stranger, she came and sat face and face with him and looked straight in his eyes. As if to say that was how it was.)

Bazam mein ous kay roo ba roo kayoon neh khamoosh baithiaay
Ous key toe khamoshee mein bhee hai yeh he mudoaa keh youn

In her company, side by side, why not sit by quietly.
For her own silence suggests and shows, as if to say,... just like so.

(Simple verse.)

Main nay kaha keh bazm e naaz chaiyay ghair say tahee
Soun kay sitam zareef nay mujh ko utha diya keh youn

Said I, that decent company, should be free of strangers.
Hearing this she made me go, as if to say,... just like so.

(Simple verse. Does not need further elaboration.)

Mujh say kaha jo yar nay jatay hain housh kis turrah
Deikh kay meree bay khudee chulnay lagi hava keh youn

She enquired of me, how do one's senses go?
Seeing my state of stupor, the breeze began to blow,
as if to say,... Just like so.

(The beloved asked of the poet as to how does one get so stupefied. Seeing him in such a state a soft breeze went by as if to tell her how quickly and quietly one looses sense and sensibility.)

Kub mujhay kooaye yar mein rehnay ki waza yaad thee
Aaina dar bun gayee hairat e nuksh e paa keh youn

When did I remember the etiquette to live in a lover's lane.
My gait reflected my anxious state, as if to say,... just like so.

(When ever the poet went to the lovers lane he became unsteady in his walk.)

Gar taray dil mein hoe khayal wasal mein shouq ka zaval
Mauj muheeth e aab mein maray hai dast o paa keh youn

Were your heart to reflect, upon loss of desire, at the moment of peak.
A wave, in an all engulfing ocean, struggles with hands and feet
as if to say,... just like so.

(In the mighty ocean of desire one tends to forget the measure of its intensity and completely loses ones identity, just as if a wave keeps up a struggle to keep afloat in the depth of an ocean.)

Joe yeh kahay keh rekhta kayun keh hoe rashk e farsee
Gufta e Ghalib eak bar purhh kay ousay suna keh youn

Were one to say, how can Persian be envious of Urdu?
Read out to him a Ghalib's verse, as if to say,... just like so

(Persian had been the lingua franca of India, and the inspiration for all writers and poets before the rise of Urdu. Ghalib took Urdu to such heights in both prose and poetry that he has the right to claim that Persian now feels jealous of it.)

GILA HAI SHOUQ KO DIL MAIN BHEE TANGI E JAA KA

Gila hai shoaq ko dil main bhee tangi e jaa ka
Gohar main mehav hua istraab darya ka

Desire complains of lack of space, even in the heart.
The tumult of the sea gets absorbed In a pearl, and becomes its part.

(For those who feel and say that there is so much to desire and not enough place in the heart to store it, the poets points to the fact that the ocean's entire radiance gets reflected in the pearl of a sea shell.)

Yeh jaanta houn keh tou aur pasikh e maktoob (pasikh= jawaab),
Magar sitamzada houn zooq e khama farsa ka (khama= qalam),
(farsa=Tabah karnay wala)

This I know that, you will surely write a reply.
My fear is the might of the pen and its dye. (ink)

(The poet is convinced that the beloved will reply his letters, he however, fears their tone and content.)

Hina e pa e khizan hai bahaar agar hai yehhe
Dawaam kulfat e khatir hai aaiysh duniya ka (dawaam= hameshgee),
(kulfat=ranj, takleef)
(khatir=jigar, kaleja)

If this is spring, then It is the colour, off the autumn's feet.
The eternal pain and woe, is in fact the gist,
of the worldly pleasures, and its treat.

(The poet says that spring is really a shade of the season of autumn, as all the suffering and pain in the world is reaction or the outcome of the enjoyment and frolicking.)

Gham e firaaq main takleef sair e baagh neh doo
Mujhay dimag naheen khanda hahay bayjaa ka
(khanda= hansee, Mazakh, shookhee)

I am in a sad and pensive state, do not coax me for a garden stroll.
Am in no mood, for jest or a happy roll.

(Simple and self contained)

Hanooz mahrumeeay husan ko tarasta hoon
Karay hai herbun e mu daam chasham e beena ka

Ever writhe in the desire and longing, for beauty's view.
The root of every hair of mine, acts like the eye, and looks for it too.

(The poet's standard of beauty is very high and keeps waiting to get a view of satisfaction. The parts of his body too keep the vigil and each one keeps a look out as if they too were the eyes.)

Dil ousko pehlay he naaz o adda say day baithay
Humay dimag kahaan husan kay taqaza ka

Gave her the heart already, with much hope and yearning.
We do not know a polite way, To ask for it's returning.

(Quite self explanatory).

GILA HAI SHOUQ KO DIL MAIN BHEE TANGI E JAA KA

Neh kayeh keh girya bah miqdaar e hasrat e dil hai
Maree nigah main hai jama o kharch darya ka

Do not say that tears are a measure of my heart's spree.
For the scale of my sight, weighs the ups and downs of the whole sea.

(The poet says the tears flowing from his eyes are no measure of his sorrow, he can cry an ocean.)

Falak ko daikh kay karta houn ous ko yaad Asad
Jafa main ous ke hai andaaz karfarma ka

When I see the sky O' Asad, I remember her.
For her torturous ways reflect, those that the Heavens too prefer.

(Self explanatory verse.)

HAI BASKAY HER EIK OUNKAY ISHARAE MEIN NISHAN AUR

Hai baskay her eik ounkay isharae mein nishan aur
Kartay hein muhabbat toe guzarta hai gumaan aur

In every hint of their's is but, a varied signal.
When they express love, it seems a different ritual.

(The beloved is quite dubious, for she says one thing but means another. Even when she expresses love it somehow seems disclaim or anger.)

Ya rub na woh sumjhaay hain na sumjhain gay meri baath
Dae aur dil ounn ko joe na dae mujh ko zubaan aur

Oh! Lord, she does not comprehend, nor ever will acclaim.
Give to her a new heart, if not me another tongue, to proclaim.

(The poet says that it is a pity that his beloved has not ever tried to understand his utterances. He pleads to God to either give her a new heart to feel his sentiments or otherwise teach him another language to express his feelings.)

Abroo say hai kaya ous neghay naz ko paywandh
Hai teer muqarrar magar ous ki hai kamaan aur

What link is there, between that fiery eyed and the refined.
Though select is the arrow, yet her bow is un- defined.

(The beloved is full of fury of passion and does not know self-control. She keeps shooting fiery glances in every direction, oblivious of the fact that her killer instincts have already made the poet a target.)

Tum sheher main hoo too hamian kaya gham jab uthayn gay
Layayan gay bazaar say jaa kar dil o jan aur

As you are in the city, what is there to regret.
We can always get a new heart and soul, from the market.

(The background to this verse is that the poets love was a woman of ill-repute who was an accessible commodity. He thus feels this type of love is like a tradable affair, easily available in the market place.)

Herchand subukdast huaye buth shikani mein
Hum hein to abhi rahh mein hai sangg giran aur

Despite the swift-handedness and that most idols were destroyed;
As long as I remain, there is, a mighty stone to be buoyed.

(This verse is in reference to Muslim's having destroyed stone idols of the Kabah. The poet says that though all other idols and statues may have been done away with, yet as long as the lover exists the final idol or hindrance remains.)

Hai khoon-e jigar josh mein dil khool kay roota
Hootay jo kai deedah khunaba fishaan aur

Blood of my soul openly cries out of emotion;
Had I more eyes they too would shed, glittering tears of devotion.

(A fairly straightforward verse.)

Marta hoon ous aawaaz pay her chand kay sir ourh jaay
Jallad ko laykin woh kahay jaien kay haan aur

I almost die at every beckoning, and fear the head will be severed.
Yet they keep telling the hang-man that, "more punishment is deserved".

(As if the poet is in the clutches of the executioner and at every call he fears that the sword will sever his head, but the beloved insists that more torture should be meted out before the final blow.)

Loogoon ko hai khursheed-e jehantaab ka dhooka
Her rose dikhata hoon mein eik daagh-e nihan aur

People think it is the burning sun, and are deceived.
Every day I show to them, the new wound I received.

(The wounds he receives remain fresh and glowing like the burning sun.)

Daytaa na agar dil tumhein laytaa koe dum chaein
Kartaa, joe na martaa, koye dinn aah o fughaan aur

Were I not to give you the heart, I may have had some ease.
Had I not died, would have lamented longer with the tease.

(The poet is repenting the fact that he fell in love and that the giving of his heart is the reason for his troubles. For, had he not died he would have lamented even longer due to the suffering.)

Paa-tay nahin jub raah too charhh jatay hein naalay
Ruktee hai maeri taabba too hootei hai rawaan aur

When the drains are blocked, they rise and swell.
My nature upon obstruction, however,flows much too well.

(The poet is comparing and contrasting his nature and the drains. For, when there is no outlet for the water in the drains their level rises, but the poets nature is such that the more it is subjugated or obstructed the better it flows.)

Hain aur bhee dunya mein sukhanwar bohat achay
Khaytay hein kay Ghalib ka hai andaaz-e bayaan aur

There are a number of other good poets on the earth;
Yet it is said that Ghalib's diction, sure has a different worth.

(A simple verse.)

HAR AIK BAAT PAY KEHTAY HOE TUM KAY TOO KAYA HAI

Har aik baat pay kehtay hoe tum kay too kaya hai
Tum hee kahooe keh yeh andaaz-e guftagoo kaya hai

At every word you say 'who in hell are you'?
Ask you yourself, if this is the right thing to do?

(The poet is addressing the beloved who is a temperamental person and who so often picks at the poet. Here the poet is just pointing this out to her.)

Neh sholay mein yeh karishma, neh barq mein yeh ada.
Koi bataoo keh who shookh tundkhoo kaya hai.

Neither the flame has this miracle, nor lightening such intensity.
Will someone tell me the true nature of this spoilt beauty.

(Here the poet is pointing towards the temper and the mercurial nature of the beloved.)

Yeh rashk hai keh who hoota hai humsukhan tum say
Wagarna khoof e budamooze a udoo kaya hai

The jealousy is of the fact that he so sweetly, to you speaks.
For otherwise what's to fear the topic of the rival's speech.

(The poet is jealous of the fact that the rival speaks sweetly to his beloved, for otherwise he does not care or fear the topic they talk about.)

Chipak raha hai badan par lahoo say parahan
Hamari jaeb ko abb hajat-e rafoo kaya hai.

With the clotting of blood the cloth to the body gets attached.
What need is there, for the torn pocket, to be stitched or patched.

(The pocket does not need to be patched because it has got repaired itself due to the clotting of the blood.)

Jala hai jism jehan, dil bhi jal gaya hooga
Kuraeedtay hoe joe abb rakh, justojoo kaya hai.

Where the body got consumed, the heart too, there must have burnt.
Poking now the ashes, pray alas! What you hope to have learnt?

(It seems the heart itself has been burnt along with the body, and consumed in the waiting. Now there is no use looking for them in the ashes .)

Ragoon mein daurtay phirnay kay hum naheen qaaiyal
Jub aankh hee say neh tapka too phir lahoo kaya hai

Galloping forth in the veins, does not impress us.
When the blood can't drop from the eye, why then all the fuss.

(The poet is addressing the rush of blood in his veins. He is not impressed by this. For, according to him it should have been shed as tears due to the intensity of pain, in order to make an impression on him.)

Who cheez jis kay liaye hum ko hoo bahisht azeez
Sivaye bada-e gulfaam-e mushkboo, kaya hai.

The thing for which, to us is heaven so dear.
What is it, but, the flower laden radiance in the air.

(The reality of heaven, according to the poet, is nothing but just a sweet smell, like the radiance of flowers.)

Piyoon sharab, agar khum bhi daekh loon doe chaar.
Yeh sheeshah o qadah o kooza o suboo kaya hai.

Would take a drink were I to see a bottle or two.
This glass, jug, pitcher or bowl. Why so much ado?

(Simple verse.)

Rahee neh taqat-e guftaar, aur agar hoe bhi.
Toe kis umeed pay kahiyay keh, arzoo kaya hai.

No strength remains to speak; and even if there was,
Then on what hope should one say, what was the desire's cause?

(The poet has lost strength even to speak, and even if he had it there is no hope, and he sees no chance for the fulfillment of his desires.)

Hua hai shah ka musahib, phira hai itraataa
Wagarna shaher mein Ghalib ke aabroo kaya hai

Has become the king's courtier, and full of pride goes forth.
For otherwise in the city, truly what else is Ghalib's worth.

(The poet his taunting himself for showing off because he has befriended the king. For, otherwise he sees no reason for the pride.)

HAIRAN HOON DIL KO ROOUN KEH PITOON JIGAR KO MAIN

Hairan hoon dil ko rooun keh pitoon jigar ko main.
Maqdoor hoe toe saath rakhoon nuahgar ko main.

Wonder if I should

weep my heart out, or beat up the soul.
Were I able, I would employ, The catharsesist for console.

(The poet's intensity of pain is such that he is confounded as to what to do, cry out or hit his head against the wall. Those who could afford it used to employ professional wailers (catharsesists), whose job it was to narrate the tragic incident over and over again and make the people cry. This act of catharses had the affect of relieving the feeling of sadness and pain.)

Chora na rashk nay, keh teray ghar ka naam loon.
Her eik say poochta hoon keh jayoon kidhar ko main.

Envy has got me down, can't even think of visiting your home.
Everyone I meet, I ask, In which lane should I roam.

(Simple verse, self contained)

Jana para raqeeb kay dar pur hazar baar,
Aay Kaash janta naa teray rahguzar ko main.

A thousand times I had to pass by the rivals abode.
Ah! Would , that I had not known Your houses road.

(Self explanatory verse)

Hai qaya joe kuskay bundhiyay, meri bala daray.
Qaya jaanta naheen houn tumarahee kumar ko main.

What is there to tighten. It's no worry of mine.
Do I not know, You have a delicate waistline?

(The poet is saying that he is not moved by the beloved's threat of self torture. He says he knows the extent of her courage.)

Lo who bhi kehtay hain keh Yeh bay nangonaam hai.
Yeh jaanta agar toe lutataa neh ghar ko main.

See, even she is apt to say, that he is nameless and fameless.
Were I to know this, I wouldn't part with my lot and become homeless.

(The poet sacrificed his all for his love, but now even the beloved says he is worthless. Had he known this would happen he would not have let everything go.)

Chalta hoon thori door her eik taizrou kay saath.
Pechanta naheen hoon abhee rehabar ko main.

I walk a short distance, with every fast paced walker.
Don't distinguish yet, between a leader and a stalker.

(This is a rather easy verse.)

Khawahish ko aahmaqoon nay parastish diya qaraar
Kaya poojhta hoon ous butay baydaad ghar ko main

Desire has been named worship by these foolish people.
Do they think I actually worship, the ruthless idol's steeple.

(Self contained verse.)

Phir baykhudee main bhool gaya rah e koo e yar.
Jataa wagarna eik din apnee khabar ko main.

Then in my senselessness I forgot the way to the lover's lane.
For otherwise I'd go to enquire, If they still know my name.

(The intensity of love has made the lover forget even himself.)

Ghalib Khuda karay keh sawar e samand e naaz,
Daykhoon , Ali bahadar e Aala gohar ko main.

Ghalib, may God grant the view, of the rider and the horse.
And that, I see Ali the brave, full of his jewels of gallant force.

(Here the poet is praying for a vision of spiritual enlightenment and a view of the courageous Ali, the cousin of the Prophet.)

HASAD SAY DIL AGAR AFSURDA HAI ...

Hasad say dil agar afsurda hai garam-e tamasha hoe
Keh chasham-e tang shaid kasarat-e nazara say waa hoe

If jealousies have saddened the heart, get absorbed in the din, but stay serene.
The narrowed view may perhaps, broaden by the abundance of the scene.

(When one gets jealous one gets sad too and the vision gets restricted and one sees only what the feelings allow. The poet is advising a deeper view of the scene, for then perhaps the real reason of the jealousies may become apparent and it may be overcome.)

Baqadaray hasarat-e dil chahiay zoaq-e maasi bhi
Bharoon yak gosha-e daman gar aab-e haft darya hoe

To gauge the heart's yearning, essential is to know wines, and why they please.
Will only wet the corner of my robe, were there the water of the seven seas.

(It is necessary to analyze the reason for any desire before giving in to it. However, even the entire ocean of wine will not be sufficient to whet my thirst or fulfill my desires.)

Agar woh sir o qad garmay kharam-e naaz aajavay
Kafay her khak-e gulshan shakalay qumree nala farsa hoe

If she, head to foot, vibrant demeanor of conceit, were to come in my domain;
The palm of each grain of the garden's sand,
Like the nightingale, would wail and complain.

(The poet's beloved is so enchanting and at the same time so provoking that he feels that were she to come, every pore of his body will cry out in pain due to the intensity of love.)

HAVIS KO HAI NISHAT E KAR KAYA KAYA

Havis ko hai nishat e kar kaya kaya
Na ho marna to jinay ka maza kaya

What all is the quest of greed to fulfill a desire.
Life would be no fun, if at last it did not expire.

(One's greed leads to putting in endless efforts to achieve its wishes. But if every desire was to be achieved or be certainly achievable, there would be no fun. One would become lax in efforts if the outcome is certain. Life itself, would lose its meaning and charm if there were no end to it and if death were never to come; Or, if its time is known with certainty, one would become relaxed in effort if the outcome was known).

Tajahil paeshgi say muddaa kaya
Kahan tak aey sara pa naaz kaya kaya

What is meant by ignoring even before we meet.
How much more pretence, oh! Head to foot conceit.

(The poet is questioning his beloved's pretence and ignoring of him, and her teasing ways.)

Nawazish hai beja dekhta hoon
Shikayat hai rangeen ka gila kaya

I watch and see, the undue showering of grace,
Why then complain of her frolicking, showy ways.

(The poet says he is observing and perhaps enjoying the excessive attention he gets sometimes. On the other hand why should one worry if the beloved's mood changes and takes a sudden turn?)

Nigahaey bay mahaba chahta hoon
Taghaful hai tamkeen aazma kaya

My wish is, she would give me an unhesitant gaze.
Why then the painful neglect, she flings my ways.

(The poet is hoping and desirous of the beloved's tender and loving glances all the time, why then he gets refusal and neglect from her?)

Faroogh e shoola e khas, yak nafas hai
Hawis ko paas e namoos e wafa kaya

The flicker of the flame of khas, Is but for an instant.
Why would lust befriend decency, for more than just a moment?

(The sweet smell of the burning scented wood (khas) is just temporary , so is the decency of a greedy person; for once his motive has been achieved he quietly glances and moves the other way?.)

Nafas, maujj e muheet e baykhudee hai
Taghaful hai saaqi ka gila kaya

Time is a wave In the depth of oblivion.
Why then complain of the saqi's lack of attention.

(Here Ghalib gives an original concept of time. He says time seems to be just a disturbance in the calm sea of everlasting tranquility; a temporary birth of consciousness in the void of unconscious oblivion. This idea is far ahead of its own time, and its meaning and beauty is enhanced if seen in the light of the theory of relativity, which was propounded by Einstein about a hundred years later. Delving a little further on the thought, time seems to have started at the moment the Deity wished to seek Itself in a conscious manner i.e. at the instant It thought of becoming a consciously 'Conscious Being'. Waking up from 'Dormancy' to 'Enlightenment', or becoming conscious of the beauty of Its own creative ability, and then being desirous to show it to the world. { This concept has been discussed in greater detail in my essay, ' Nature of a Natural Deity'.} In the second stanza says Ghailb says that, ' does it really matter if the saqi (the beautiful tavern hostess) forgot to pass a round of drinks' ? In other words we should not complain if the Creator turns His attention momentarily from our needs, and seems to be disinterested in us.)

Dimag e iterr e parahan naheen hai
Gham e awargee haaye saba kaya

When even the scent on the dress does not please,
Why then the sadness at the frolic of the morning breeze.

(The beloved's sensitivity can not even stand the perfume of the robe. Why then does she seem to bother about the soft unfaithful morning breeze ?)

Dil e har qatra hai sazay analbaher
Hum ous kay hain humara poochna kaya

The heart of every drop by itself, is in tune with the sea.
We are for her and her alone, so what ask of we?

(The poet says that a sensitive heart is capable of listening to the tune of the universe, and that since the beloved has acclaimed the lover there is no limit to his joy. The other connotation of the verse is that each one of us is in actuality a part of the Whole i.e. We are for God and God alone , so why worry what the end will be ?)

Muhaba qaya hai, mein zamin, idhar daiykh
Shaheedan e nigah ka khoon baha kaya

What's your fear trust me, look my way;
Those who die by killer glances, get no blood money as repay.

(The poet reassures the beloved and guarantees that she should not fear looking at him, for even if he dies by the magic of her glances, no blood money (which is an Islamic injunction) will be due for such death.)

Sunn aye garatgaray jinsay wafa, sunn
Shakist e qeemat e dil ki sada kaya

Listen O destroyer of the sense of faith, just hear.
What worth is the call of a defeated heart? – my dear.

(The beloved is being called the destroyer of faith, for all sensibility and belief is lost when the poet sees her, and he surrenders his heart and soul to her. For, once subdued and conquered such, what is the value of all his hue and cries.)

Kiya kis nay jigardaree ka dava?
Shakeeb e khatir e ashiq bahala kaya

Who, in the agony of love did Alas! prevail.
So! patience in the service of love, to what avail?

(No one can bear and survive the pain and torture of love and be a conqueror of it. Why then should one be patient and bear all the torture?)

Yeh qatil, wada sabar azmaa qayoon?
Yeh kafir, fitna e taqat ruba kaya

This killer promise, bear it with patience – try?
This sinister evil full of power – why?

(The poet says the beloved wants him to promise to bear with patience the days of separation. This (pain of separation) is a powerful evil, how can one fight it?)

Bala e jaan hai Ghalib ous ke har baat
Ibarat kaya, isharat kay, aada kaya.

Most intricate, O ghalib, Is his every talk.
What a script, what hints and what mock.

(This seems to be the poet's admiration of his own verse and poetry, though in the garb of praise of his own beloved; because the talk is so illusive, the words so intricate and full of pun and mock.)

HAZAROON KHAWASISHAIN AYESI KEH HER KHAWAHISH PAY DUM NIKLAY

Hazaron khawahishain ayesi keh her khawahish pay dum niklay
Boath niklay meray armaan laykin phir bhi kum niklay

A thousand wishes such, each takes away one's breath so much.
Though many desires were achieved, many remained unfulfilled as such.

(The poet says that one has so many desires in life, and that the more they are fulfilled the more one wishes.)

Daray qayoon mera qatil kya rehgaya ous ki gardan pur
Who khoon jo chasham e tar say umr bhr youn dum ba dum niklay

What does my killer fear? Is it on his neck there lies;
Blood, that oozes out life-long , from my brimming eyes.

(The poet is being sarcastic and is teasing her killer for being afraid of the blood stain on his collar, in other words the bad name she will get. He says that it is the same tears of blood that he has been weeping all his life.)

Nikalna khuld say Adam ka suntay ayae hain lekin
Bohat beabroo ho kur taray kunchay say hum niklay

We have always heard about Adam's woeful exit from the heaven.
But with much ignominy, we were expelled from your cabin.

(Adam is said to have been shamefully removed from paradise on account of his mistake. The poet says that his exit from the beloved's door was even worse.)

Bharam khuljayae ga zalim teray qamat ki darazee ka
Agar iss turaa e parpaych o kham ka paych o kham niklay

All truth will be exposed of your stature and your gown;
If only the ups and downs of your head-gear, loses its up to down.

(The head gear of the elite in the east is usually decorated by a fan like extension on the cap. This is called the 'turra'. The bigger the stature the higher the turra. This turra is kept stiff with starch. This gives the person a position of pride. The poet says if the starch of the turra is lost it will become limp and so will the pride.)

Magar likhwayay koi ousko khut to humsay likhwayay
Hui subh aur ghar say kaan par rakh kur qalam niklay

But, if one were to send her a letter, we should be asked to write.
For, as the dawn breaks every morn,
we perch a pen on the ear, and from the house alight.

(Self explanatory)

Hui iss daur main mansoob mujh say bada ashaami
Phir aya who zamana jo jehan main jaam o jum niklay

In this time and age, drunkenness became associated with me.
There will comes a time when Jamshed's wine cup, common fashion would be.

(The poet is predicting that although he is being blamed as a drunkard by his compatriots, the time is not far when every house will have some one or the other who will take to drinking.)

Hui jin say tawaqaah khastgee ki daad panay ki
Who hum say bhi zayadha khasta taegh e situm niklay

On whom we pinned hopes for praise of endurance in our misery;
They were seen to be even more poverty stricken, than we.

(The poet had hoped that his friend will complement him on his patience and endurance of adversity, but he found out that he was himself poorer than he.)

Mohabat main naheen hai farqq jinay aor murnay ka
Ousi ko daykh kar jeetay hain jis kafir peh dum niklay

In love there is no distinction between life and death.
One lives for the same heretic, seeing whom, one loses all breath.

(Love leaves no difference in life and death. One who is the cause of ones death is also the same person who one lives to see.)

Khuda kay wastay purdah na Kabay ka uttha waiz
Khaheen ayesa na hoe yaan bhi wohee kafir sanam niklay

For God's sake O' pious one do not raise the Kabah's curtain.
May be there too, is the stone for idols, one cannot really be certain.

(The poet is taunting the pious person not to lift the curtain of the Kaba, for he says that it too may turn out to be an idol, because it is also made of stone.)

Khaan maykhanay ka darwaaza Ghalib aur khaan waiz
Pur itna jantain hain kal who jaata thaa keh hum niklay

Where be the pious, O' Ghalib, and where the tavern's way.
However, this we know, that he entered as we were leaving, yesterday.

(The poet is pointing out the fact that perhaps it is not possible to find a pious person at the door of the tavern. But he himself saw such a one enter the tavern as he was leaving the other day.)

HUSAN E MAI GARCHAY BAHANGAM E KAMAL ACHA HAI

Husan e mai garchay bahangam e kamal acha hai
Iss say mera mai khursheed e jamal acha hai

Though for restless talent, the effect of wine is beautiful.
Better is my beloved's glow, like the sun at its glory, full.

(Ghalib says that wine is good to tame the uncontrolled restlessness. But better than that is the intoxication of the beauty of his beloved, who glows like the sun at noon.)

bosa datay naheen aur dil pay hai her lahaza nigah
jee main kehatay hain keh muft aayae to maal acha hai

Does not give a kiss, yet, every moment eye's the heart.
Whispers to herself that, — For free, it wouldn't be a bad start.

(a simple verse, does not need elaboration).

Aur bazaar say layayay agar toot gaya
Saghar e Jam say mera jam e safaal acha hai

Shall get another from the market If this one were to break.
Better, than Jamshed's jeweled cup, Is mine of earthenware make.

(Simple verse but with much deeper contotation)

Bay talab dain toe maza iss main sava milta hai
Woh gada jis koe nah hoe khooaye sawal acha hai

If given without asking, there is double the fun.
A silent needy is better, than a begging one.

(If a needy person asks repeatedly it becomes irritating and one does not like to give. To a silent beggar one quietly gives without hesitation.)

Daikhiay paatay hain ushaasq butoon say kaya faiz
Eik barhaman nay kaha hai keh yeh saal acha hai

See what benefit, we may get from idol lovers.
A brahaman predicts that, this year may be full of flowers.

(Simple verse.)

Oun kay daykhay say jo aajatee hai munh par ronaq
Wooh sumajhtay hain keh beemar ka haal acha hai

Seeing them, that, The face brightens and spirits swell;
They think that, The patient is hearty and well.

(Simple verse.)

Hum sukhan tashay nay Farhaad ko Shireen say kaha
Jis tarhay ka keh kisi main hoe kamal acha hai

Mountain planer Farhad said to his Shireen;
Whatever talent one has, Is never mean.

(Farhad was a mountain digger and loved a very beautiful girl Shireen. He is consoling her that any talent one possesses is better than no talent at all.)

Qatra dariya main joe mil jayay toe dariya hoe jayay
Kaam acha hai wooh jis ka keh faal acha hai.

A drop that joins the sea, becomes itself the sea.
An act that has a good omen, good itself will be.

(Another simple verse.)

Hum ko maaloom hai janat ke haqiqat laykin
Dil kay khush rakhnay ko Ghalib yeh khayal acha hai

We know the reality of paradise, Ghalib, yet;
To keep the heart pleased, it's a good thought to beget.

(Simple verse yet so profound.)

IBN E MARIAM HUA KARAY KOOIE

Ibn-e Mariam Hua Karay kooie
Meray dukh kee dawa karay kooie

One maybe the son of Mary;
Who can cure me, of my malady.

(The son of Mary i.e. Jesus was said to cure people of their illnesses. So, the poet is calling out and saying that he will be convinced of the power of the son of Mary only if he will cure him of his malady.)

Sharah O aaieen parr madaar sahiee
Aasay qatil ka kaya karay kooie

May well be religious, or even lawful.
What can one do, with a killer so awful.

(Although the person who killed the poet may well be within the limits of law, yet she is a killer and how can a killer be excused for the crime.)

Chaal jaisay karri kaman ka teer
Dil maein asay kay jaa karay kooie

Gait, as a bows straight shot arrow.
In her heart, should someone, make a burrow.

(The poet's love is full of conceit, rather blunt, and direct in approach. Now the challenge is to subdue such a person and win over her heart.)

Baat par waan zaban katthi hai
Wooh kahain aur suna karay kooie

The speech is cut short in her presence there.
She alone to continue to speak, and all others to listen with care.

(The beloved is rather talkative and does not let anyone else speak and cuts short if interrupted.)

Naa suno gar bura khahay kooie
Naa kahoo gar bura karay kooie

Do not heed if someone says things bad.
Don't complain when wronged and you feel sad.

(This is the poet's advice from experience.)

Rook loo gar ghalat chalay kooie
Baksh doo gar khata karay kooie

Restrain him who wrongly treads along.
Forgive his faults, who does you wrong.

(Another piece of advise from the poet.)

Koan hai joe nahin hai hajat mandh
kis ki hajat rawa karay kooie

Who's there that's not in want or need?
Whose want can one fulfill indeed?

(The poet says that each and every one is in need of something or the other, and it is impossible to fulfill every ones desires.)

Kaya kia Khizar nay Sikandar say
Abb kisay rehnuma karay kooie

What did Khizar do to Alexander.
Who should be taken guide, I wonder?

(If the guide led even the most powerful astray then how can anyone trust anyone to lead the way.)

Bakk raha hoon junoon mein kaya kaya kutch
Kutch na sumjhay Khuda karay kooie

What all, in my senselessness, I do utter.
May God, no one understand my mutter.

(The poet is reflecting on his own utterances and feels they may be of no use to anyone.)

Jab tawaqaa he uthh gaie Ghalib
Kayuun kisi ka gila karay kooie

When expectation is lost and gone.
Why should one, O` Ghalib complain anon.

(When relations get sour one loses interest and expectations of another, then what is the use of complaining to him.)

ISHRAT E QATRA HAI DARIYA MEIN FANA HOO JANA

Ishrat-e qatra hai dariya mein fana hoo jana
Dard ka hudh say guzarna hai dawa hoo jana

The ecstasy for every drop, Is to become one with the sea;
When pain exceeds all limits, it becomes a remedy.

(This opening verse points to the similarities in opposites, the correlation of the beginning with the end and the relationships of the unrelated phenomena. This is in fact the theme of the entire poem.)

Tujh say qismat may mayree surat-e qufal-e abjad
Tha likha baat kay buntay he juda hoo jana

My destiny with you, like the combination lock;
Was to separate, the instant all elements ticked like a clock.

(The latch and bolt of a combination lock separate only when the numbers match. Here the poet says that the matching of their natures did not suit lady luck, and destiny set them apart the moment all things harmonized in their relationship.)

Dil hua kashmakash-e charah-e zahmat may tamam
Mitt gaya ghisnay mein iss Uqad-e ka wa hoo jana

The heart was consumed in the routine troubles of life.
The knot's ability to untie was lost, in the rubbing and strife.

(The knot is easy to open when fresh and crisp. The old worn out knot is far more difficult to untie. Similarly a heart trampled by the world is difficult to excite and arouse.)

Ab jafa say bhi hain mehroom hum Allah Allah
Iss qadar dushman-e arbaab-e wafa hoo jana

We are now, deprived even of torture – Lord Oh! Lord.
The extent to which the once beloved has developed animosity and discord.

(The beloved who showered love and affection has turned her attention and the poet says that now she is not even ready to detest or even torture.)

Zuff say gar yeh mubaddal bedaam e sard hua
Bawaar aya humain pani ka hawa hoo jana

Weakness set in by weeping, such that, the warmth of the body came to pass;
This surely made me comprehend, how water cools when it turns to gas.

(The extreme weakness due to endless crying results in the loss of even the warmth of life, just the way the evaporation of water due to heat, results in the cooling of the surroundings.)

Dil say mitna terri angushatt-e hinai ka khayaal
Hoo gaya goshtt say nakhoon ka juda hoo jana

Removal from the heart of the thought of your finger, 'henna-dyed';
Became as if it were the separation, of the nail from the hide.

(To try and forget the sight of the beloved's beautiful fingers, dyed with henna, became as painful as if a nail is being pulled out from its skin.)

Hai mujhay abr-e bahari ka baras kar khulna
Roottay roottay gham-e furquat mein fana hoo jana

The clearing of the sky after heavy monsoon precipitation;
Is akin to perishing, in endless weeping of separation.

(The calm after a monsoon storm seem like the silence of death after wailing and crying and then its passing away.)

Gar naheen nighat-e gul ko teray kunchay ki havis
Qayuun hai gard-e rah e joolan-e sabah hoo jana

If the scent of the flower is not desirous of your court yard's ease;
Why then does the dust of the path acquire swiftness in the morning breeze.

(The poet questions the phenomena of nature where, if the scent of flowers, or in other words peace and serenity are difficult to find in the lovers lane, then why is it that hurt or pain reaches there so quickly.)

Taa kay tujh pur khulay eijaz e hawa-e saiqqal
Deikh barsaat mein sabz aainay ka hoo jana

So that you may be acquainted with the miracle of air, pure and clean.
See in the monsoon, how, even the mirror turns green.

(The idea here is that the environment affects every thing. A good environment makes one happy, so much so that in the monsoon even the mirror reflects and shows only greenness.)

Bakhshay hai jalwa-e gul zuaq-e tamasha Ghalib
Chasham ko chahiay her rung mein waa hoo jana

The beauty of the flower, Ghalib, enhances the aesthetics of the scene.
The eye should be able to adapt to every shade, and stay serene.

(The poet leaves here with a message that though good times please everyone, one should be able to bear all situations with courage, fortitude, and patience and stay calm.)

ISS BAZM MAIN MUJHAY NAHEEN BANTI

Iss bazm main mujhay naheen banti haya kiyay
Baytha raha agarchay isharay hua kiyay

No shyness befits me In this company.
Remained seated, though, many hints were flung at me.

(The poet sat in the company of prostitutes and dancing girls where he felt out of place because of his decent ways. Yet he kept his station despite teases and uncomfortable situations.)

Dil he toe hai siasat e darban say dar gaya
Main aur jayoon dar say teray bin sada kiyay

It is but a heart, got shaken by the fear of the guard.
Or else without beckoning at your door, would I depart?

(The poet got intimidated by the ferocity of the portal guard of the lovers lane and could not even beckon the beloved from the door.)

Rakhta phiroon hoon kharqa e sajada rahen e mai
Muddat hui hai davat e aab o hava kiyay

I offer the 'shirt on my back', as ransom for some wine.
Its been an age since I had a relaxed, 'drink and dine'.

(The thirst for a drink is so intense that the poet is willing to offer even the shirt on his back as there is nothing else of value left to give.)

Bay sarfa he guzartee hai hoe garchay umar e Khizer
Hazrat bhe kal kahaingay keh hum kaya kiya kiyay

Even without spending, it passes, may well be the life of a guide.
Even he will wonder on the morrow, what he did not do,
and to what, did he abide.

(Life gets consumed without spending whether one likes it or not, be it of a rouge or a saint. And each will wonder as to where it went and what he achieved in its span.)

Maqdoor hoe to khaak say poochoon kay aye laeem
Tou nay whoo ganjhai garan maya kaya kiyay

If power I have, I'd ask the earth, O' you miserly one;
With all jewels and treasures of the world, what indeed you have done?

(This is a self explanatory verse and does not need elaboration.)

Kis rose thomatain neh tarasha kiyay udoo
Kis din humaray sir peh neh araay chala kiyay.

Which day passed that, the rivals did not complain.
What moment lapsed, that on our head, a dangling sword did not remain.

(The poet is lamenting the fact that not a day passed when the rivals did not defame him and he was blamed and discredited. He lived in perpetual fear of their attack.)

Sohbat main gair ke neh paree hoe kahaeen yeh kho
Dainay laga hai bosa baghair ilteja kiyay

In the company of strangers, may this habit would not have formed.
Has started to give kisses, without asking or being informed.

(The poet is pleasantly surprised at the behaviour of his beloved who seems to have acquired the habit of showing affection without hesitation or request. He feels she must have acquired it in the company of strangers.)

Zid ke hai aur baat magar kho buree nahin
Bhoolay say ous nay sainkroon waday wafa kiyay

Stubbornness is another matter, but this habit is not at all amiss;
In forgetfulness and unknowingly, she fulfilled a hundred and one promise.

(The subject matter is similar to the previous verse.)

Ghalib tum hee kahoo keh mailay ga javab kaya
Mana keh tum kaha kahay aur whoo suna kiyay

O! Ghalib guess yourself and say, what reply will she be making.
For though you kept on talking, she listened without speaking.

(The poet is wondering as to what his fate will be for the beloved kept listing to all he said without giving any indication.)

JOOR SAY BAAZ AAYAY PER BAAZ AAYAN KAYA

Joor say baaz aayay per baaz aayan kaya
Khaytay hain hum tujh ko munh dikhlayan kaya

Abstained from torture, but how can it be so?
By saying, " how to you, can I, my face show" ?

(After having tortured so long the beloved is ashamed and says, how can she show her face to the lover? But in not showing of the face is the greatest torture for him.)

Raat din gardish main hain saat aasman
Hoe rahay ga kutch na kutch ghabrayan kaya

The seven skies are in flight, day and night.
Some thing is bound to happen why should we fright?

(The heavens are busy moving and planning through the passage of time. Some thing is sure to come out of it, so why the worry?)

Laag hoe toe ous koe hum sumjhayan lagaoo
Jub neh hoe kutch bhi toe dhoka Kahayan kaya

If there is traction, we may think it to be attraction.
When there is nothing, what else is there, but distraction?

(Simple verse.)

Ho liayay kayoon namabar kay sath sath
Ya rub apnay khat ko hum phonchayan kaya

We do accompany the mail man, thitherto?
Oh lord! Should we deliver, our own letter too?

(Simple verse.)

Mauj e khoon sir say guzar hee kayoon neh jayay
Mur gayay pur daykhiay dikhlayan kaya

The wave of blood may well pass over the head;
Though we perished, yet what to show, as done or said?

(The poet says that he may have drowned in the flow of the river of torture and pain, yet he left nothing behind to show for.)

Puchtay hain wooh keh Ghalib koan hai
Koi batlaoo keh hum batlain kaya

They ask about Ghalib, as to who is he?
Will someone tell us, what should the answer be?

(Simple verse does not require elaboration.)

JUNOON TOHMAT KASHAY TASKEEN NA HO GAR SHADMANI KI

Junoon tohmat kashay taskeen na ho gar shadmani ki
Namak pashay kharash e dil hai lazat zindagni ki

(Shadmni ko taskeen hoti hai jubkeh wooh junoon ko apni kee hui ghalatioon ka ilzam dati hai, keh main nay yeh kaam junoon ki halat main kia, warna main toe asa kaam karnay wala adami naheen hoon. Agar wooh ayasa neh karay toe lazat uthnay kay baad insan apnay ko lanat malamat karta rahay aur ayesee takleef main mubtala rahay jasay keh dil ki kisi karaash pur namak chirak diya gaya hoe. Ab iss saray masallehy main joe baat samajhnay ki hai wooh yeh keh lazzat darasaal buray kaam karnay main zayaidah hooti hai, jasaykeh sharaab pinay main yah zina karnay main. Iss amal kay baad jub iss ka asar zaiyal how jata hai aur insan koe pachtava honay lagta hai toe apnay junoon ko hee bura bhala khanay lagta ha, aur phir yoon apnay aap koe tasalli dayta hai.)

Were infatuation not to bear insults, of the joys of life;
Salt on the wounds of the heart, would be the pleasure of its strife.

(Were the joys of life not to get satisfaction by insulting insanity, there would be no peace of mind. All the pleasure in life would be become the pain of repentance, as if salt was being sprinkled on an open wound of the heart.)

Kasha kesh hai haste say karay kaya sayeeay azadee
Hui zanjeer mauj e aab koe fursat rawani kee

How can struggle seek freedom, from the life and one's existence?
Has become a chain, for the wave of water, Its own freedom of subsistence.

(Struggle is an integral part of existence and one can not be free of it till the end of life itself; just as the movement in a wave is its own chain to keep it intact, for otherwise the wave will fall apart and become only drops of water, which is what its is basically made up of.)

Puss az murdan bhi diwana zirat gha e tiflaan ahi
Sharer e sang nay turbat peh mare gulfishanee ke

Even after death is crazy to see, the revered places of youth bygone.
My grave was flowered, by the sparks of its own tombstone.

(The poet, even after death, longs to visit the places of his youth. The feeling is like the sparks of the tombstone of his own grave that is spread, instead of flowers sent by someone who misses him.)

JUZ QAIS AUR KOI NA AYA BAROO E KAAR

Juz qais aur koi na aya baroo e kaar
Seharaah magar batangeay chashame husood tha

But for Qais, none gave to love, its worth or its due.
Even the wilderness was insufficient, on account of its limited view.

(The poet says that it was only Qais, (commonly known as Majnoo), that sacrificed his all in his love for Laila . The love and doting he showed is unsurpassed in the annals of infatuation. Thus he alone fulfilled the duties of a lover. Even the entire expanse of the wilderness seemed insufficient to contain Majnoo's restlessness, who roamed far and wide in search of his beloved.)

Aashuftagee nay naqsh suvaida kiya durust
Zahir hua keh daagh ka surmaya dood tha

Worries set right the impressions of life.
It became clear that, up in smoke were the assets of strife.

(The worldly woes bogged down the whole life to worthlessness. It all went to show that in the end all effort goes up in smoke.)

Tha khawaab mein khayaal ko thujj say muamla
Jub aankh khulgayee neh ziayan tha neh sood tha

The thought had dealing with you, in the dream's domain.
For when the eye did open, No interest had accrued, or any loss or gain.

(This couplet is self explanatory)

Layta hoon maktabe ghame dil mein subaq hanooz
Laykin yahee keh raft gaya aur bood tha

This lesson I take in the school of the sorrows of my heart.
That 'gone was to go' and --' was had to depart.'

(The diction of the verse is simple yet its philosophy is immense. It does not require much elaboration, but deep thought.)

Dhanpa kafan nay daag e ayoub e burhaingee
Mein warna her libas mein nung o wojood tha

The shroud covered the nakedness of the defect of my substance.
For else in every garb, i was devoid of meaningful existence.

(Only after death man gets the cover of a shroud. For in life he is exposed at every turn and may not be able to hide his real nature.)

Taishay baghair mur na saka kohkan Asad
Sirgushta e khumar e rusoom o qayood tha

The mountain mover Asad, couldn't even die, without his tools.
He was so caught up in the stupor of traditions, and man made rules.

(The poet says that he was so entangled and associated with the ways and traditions of the time and society that he could not even die of his free will or without the traditional ceremony and rituals of burial -- all made by man.)

KAL KAY LIYAE KAR AAJ NA KHASST SHARAB MEIN

Kal kay liyae kar aaj na khasst sharab mein
Yeh sou e zan hai saqai e kausar kay baab mein.

For tomorrow's sake, do not be miserly, in today's drinking realm.
This is an act of doubt of the saqi, of the heaven's stream.

(The poet says that one should not put off for the next day the work of today. If one is enjoying drinks one should not be miserly in letting the flask flow, as this is a negation of the magnanimity of Heaven's gift).

Hain aaj qayun zaleel keh kal tak nah thee pasand
Gustakhi e farishta hamari janab mein.

Why are we dishonoured today, when only yesterday was rejected,
The disrespect by the angel; and our honour was projected.

(It is said that when Adam (man) was formed even angles were asked to bow before him. All bowed but Iblees (satan), who was an angle then. He refused and was reprimanded by God. Seeing the present condition of man in the world the poet laments as to why humans are so down trodden today.)

Raw mein hai raksh e omar kahaan dakhiaye thamay
Nay haath baag par hai nah paa hai rakaab mein

In full gallop is the steed of life, see where it may stoop.
Neither is the reign in hand, nor feet in stirrup's loop.

(The poet is describing the uncontrollable speed of life of those who do not have any restraints on desires. It is like a run away horse where the rider has lost the grip of the rein and the foot-hold on the stirrup.)

Itna he mujh ko apni haqeeqat say boaad hai
Jitna keh weham e ghair say hoon pacih o taab mein.

So much apart I am, from my own reality;
As perplexed is I am of another's duality.

(Ghalib says that he is perplexed by peoples behaviour and attitude, as much as he is confounded by his own existence.)

Aasal e shaheed o shahid o mashood eik hai
Hairan hoon phir mushahida hai kis hisab mein

The essence of view, viewed and viewer is the same.
Surprised than I am, why to view is a different game?

(The poet is pointing out the nature of the deity, who is Itself the View, Viewer and the Viewed. The question is then why to see It is impossible?)

Hai mushtamal namood e soor par vojood e behr
Yan kaya dahara hai qatrah o mauj o habab mein.

Apparent only in appearance, is the might of the sea.
For in a wave, that's bubbles of water, what else could there be?

(The might and fury of a thing is mostly external and outwardly. Just as a mighty wave is in reality is just bubbles of water.)

Sharam eik ada e naz hai apnay he say sahee
Hein kitnay behijab keh youn hain hijab mein.

Shyness is an act of a fanciful notion, be it with oneself.
How exposed they are, the more they seek to cover their self.

(No matter how much one dresses to cover oneself, one can not hide from ones own self.)

Aaraish e jamal say farigh nahin hanooz
Paish e nazar hai aaina daim naqaab mein

Of the enhancement of beauty, is never free alas!
In the veil, to view at all times, is a looking glass.

(This is again showing the conceited nature of man. Even when by himself one is always reviewing, planning and conniving the next move.)
Hai ghaib e ghaib jis ko samajhtay hain hum shahood
Hain khawoob mein hanooz jo jagay hain khawoob mein

Unpresent is hidden, yet manifest, to us it may seem.
In constant dream we live, though we may wake up in a dream.

(The poet is saying that this life is an illusion of existence, and though visible, is nevertheless not real, and as per Plato is a reflection of some other reality which may exist beyond our senses . It seems we go about being fully awake, yet in actuality we are in a never ending dream. We have no independence of our own and only follow the dictates of Nature.)

Ghalib nadeem dost say aati hai bouay dost
Mashgool e haq hoon bandagi e bootarab mein

Ghalib, the sweat of a friend, radiates a friendly smell.
I seek the truth of humanity, in the flavour of this earth's shell.

(If a person is friendly one can feel it by his attitude. The poet says he looks for truth all around, even in the earth's crust, its surface and external appearance – all of which are the personification of humans, because that is what they are made of.)

KAYUUN JAL GAYA NA TAAB E RUKH E YAR DEIKH KARR

Kayuun Jal gaya na taab-e rukh-e yar deikh karr
Jalta hoon apni taqqat-e deedar deikh karr

Why did I not burn on seeing the heat of her ire,
I am jealous of my own ability to bear the fire.

(The poet is admiring his own endurance and questions as to why did he not get consumed in the fiery heat of the beloved's beauty.)

Aatesh parast kehtay hain ehlay jehan mujhay
Sargarm naala hai shararbar deikh karr

The residents of the world all call me a fire-worshiper,
By seeing me lament and exclaim, on viewing the burning cinder.

(This is a continuation of the thought of the earlier verse whereby due to the poets ability of admire the fiery beauty, people think he is a fire worshiper or a Zoroastrian.)

Kaya aabroo-e ishq jehan aam ho jefa?
Rukta hoon tum ko bay sabab aazar deikh karr

How can love be kept under-cover, where selflessness is supreme;
I come to stop , when you look troubled, for no reason, it may seem.

(According to the eastern tradition of the olden days, love had to be kept hidden from the eyes of the jealous rivals. Yet on seeing the beloved disturbed for no apparent reason, the poet cannot help but question as to what is it that ails her.)

Aata hai meray qattal ko pur josh rashk say
marta hoon ous kay haath mein talwaar deikh karr

To murder, she approaches me, full of fiery passion.
Enough is for me to die, seeing a dagger in her possession.

(The beloved is as vicious as a killer who approaches with full fury, but it is enough sign of death for the lover just to see a dagger in her hand.)

Sabit hua hai gardan-e meena pay khoon-e khalkh
Larzaay hai mauj-e mai teree raftaar deikh karr

The guilt of the destruction of humanity, lies on wine and drink.
The wave in the wine-cup, however, trembles, at your swift blink.

(The drinking of wine is the cause of many a death, but the wave in the wine cup itself trembles when it sees the majestic gait of the beloved.)

Wah hasraata! keh yaar nay kheencha sitam say haath
Hum ko harees-e lazzat-e aazar deikh karr

Oh! feeling of unfulfilled desire, that, she withheld the blow,
Upon seeing me so blissfully content, in the woe.

(The poet says that just when he was getting used to and enjoying the neglectful and torturous ways of the beloved, she even stopped torturing and teasing.)

Bik jaatayhein hum aap mutha-e sukhan kay saath
Laykin aiyaar-e tabba khareedaar deikh karr

Our self, we are sold along with the chosen ware:
but, to the purchaser, who is beautiful and fair.

(Relatively easy verse.)

Zanaar bandh, saba-e sad dana toorh daal
Reh-rooh chalay hai rahh ko hamwaar deikh karr

Put away the lucky charm and break away the rosary.
The guide leads, only after seeing the path is trouble free.

(The lucky charm and the turning of the rosary are of no avail. The guide leads the caravan after making sure that the way is safe for travel)

In aabloon kay paaoon say ghabra gaya tha mein
Jee khush hua hai rahh ko pur khaar deikh karr

Was getting fed up with these blisters of my feet.
Seeing that the route is thorny, it now seems a treat.

(Simple verse.)

Girnee thee hum pay barq-e tajalee na toor pur
Deytay haim badah zarf qaddah khawar deikh karr

Ours was the destiny to be thunder-struck, not the mount of Toor.
The wine flask is only given to them, Who can hold a drink, or more.

(The poet says lightening should have struck him instead of mount Toor. He is used to bearing heavens wrath much more and so is more capable to bear pain and sorrow.)

Sir phoorna wooh Ghalib-e shooreedaa haal ka
yaad aagaya mujhay tarei diwaar deikh karr

The pounding of head by Ghalib, whose lot is naught but downfall;
came to haunt me, upon seeing your boundary wall.

(When the poet passed by the stone wall of the beloved's house he was rminded how the lover used to pound his head there.)

KISI KO DAE KAY DIL KOEE NAVASANJAY FUGHAAN QAYOON HOE

Kisi ko dae kay dil koee navasanjay fughaan qayoon hoe
Nah hoe jab dil he sinay main to phir munh main zubaan qayoon hoe

After giving someone the heart, why should one lament and complain ?
For when there is no heart in the chest,
why should the tongue in the mouth remain ?

(Ghalib is questioning the fact that when the heart is lost why not the tongue also. For then it would not be left behind to lament and complain.)

Who apni khoo na chorain gay hum apni waza qayoon badlain
Subak sir bunkay kaya puchain keh hum say sirgiran qayoon hoe

They will not give up their ego, so why change our temperament?
Why become humble and ask, the reason for their estrangement?

(When the beloved is full of pride and does not give in, why should the lover stoop down and humiliate himself, and ask about her welfare and the reason for her displeasure.)

Kiya ghamkhaar nay rusva lagay aag is mohabat ko
Na lavay taab joe gham ki who mera razdaan qayoon hoe

Friends brought me to shame; Fire of hell may such sympathy see.
He who cannot bear the pain, why should my confidant be?

(The one with who the poet shared the pain of his love's torturous tale, revealed it to the world. What use is such a friend who can not even keep a secret.)

Wafa kaisi khaan ka ishq jub sir phoorna tahera
Toe phir aay sangdil tera hi sang e aastaan qayoon hoe

What's devotion and what's love? for when the head is to pound;
Then why O stone hearted one, should it be on a boulder of your ground.

(When one has to smash ones head out of frustration why should it be done with a stone from the grounds of the beloved.)

Qafas mein mujh say roodaday chaman kehtay na darr humdum
Giri hai jis pay kal bijli who mera aashiaan qayoon hoe

In prison, do not hesitate to tell me about home, O' friend.
For, which the lightening stuck last night, why should it be my den?

(Although I am a prisoner and can do nothing about it, don't hesitate to tell me the bad news, that what the lightening struck last night, was indeed my nest.)

Yeh kehhsaktay hoe "hum dil mein nahin hain", par yeh butlaoo
Keh jub dil mein tum he tum hoe to aankhoon say nihaan
qayoon hoe

You can say "I am not in your heart" but please do tell;
that when you are all over my heart, why not in my eyes as well?

(The beloved may say that the poet has no place in her heart, yet for him she is all over his heart. So, the question is why is she not in his eyes too i.e. why can he not see her whenever he thinks about her or wishes to?)

hai jazba e dil ka shikwa daykhoo jurm kis ka hai
Neh khainchoo gar tum apnay ko kashakash darmian qayoon ho

Wrong is to blame the intensity of desire, see where the fault really lies.
For, were you not to pull aside, why between us should tension, then arise?

(It is wrong to say that the poet's over infatuation is to blame for the resistance of the beloved. The fault is actually that of the beloved, for if she is to give in easily there would be no tension at all.)

Yeh fitna aadmi ki khana weraani ko qaya kum hai
Huay tum doost jis kay dushman ous ka aasman qayoon hoe

Is this mischief not enough for man's loss and destruction;
That, whoever so you befriend, why is there need for heaven's obstruction?

(The poet says that love is enough to destroy someone. For, when one falls in love the whole world becomes his enemy.)

Yeh he hai aazmana to satana kis ko kehtay hain
Odoo kay holiaye jub tum to mera imtahaan qayoon hoe

If this is the way to test, which else is the way to misery?
For when you befriended the rival, why should then my trial be?

(Ghalib says that to become friendly with the rival is no way to try a person's patience and faithfulness.)

Kaha tum nay keh qayoon hoe ghair kay milnay mein ruswaee
Baja kehtay hoe, such kehtay hoe, phir kahoo keh han qayoon hoe

Said you, that why should meeting strangers be disgraceful and low?
Your are right, you say the truth, say again, why should it be so?

(Ghalib's intricate logic in such simple words.)

Nikala chahta hai kaam kaya taanoon say tou Ghalib
Teray bay mohur khanay say who tujh pay meharban qayoon hoe

You want, O' Ghalib to be sarcastic, and get your way.
Why, by your pinching speech, should she, towards you sway ?

(Self contained verse.)

KOI OMEED BARR NAHEEN AATI

Koi omeed barr naheen aati
Koi surat nazar naheen aati

No hope comes to fulfillment,
There seems no way , out of this ailment.

(Simple verse.)

Mauth ka eik din muaiyan hai
Neend kayuun rath bhar naheen aati

Fixed is the day and time for death.
Sleep at night, why don't I get?

(Why does one worry all the time, knowing fully well that all things come to an end and that the time for death is fixed.)

Aagay aati thi haal-e dil peh hansi
Abb kisi baath pur naheen aati

In the past, I laughed at the state of heart.
Now, I laugh at nothing -- from end to start.

(Simple verse.)

Janta hun sawaab taath o zahidh
Pur tubiut idhar naheen aati

I know the blessings of piety and prayer;
but my nature, does not lead me there.

(Simple verse no elaboration needed.)

Hai kutch ayesi he bath jo chupp hun
varna kaya bath kar naheen aati

It is some such thing, that I say naught;
For otherwise, what words have I not got.

(Some good reason holds back the poet from saying things, otherwise he can say a lot.)

Qayuun na chikhoon kay yaad kurtaey hain
Meri awaaz gar nahien aati

Why should I not shout, for they miss me;
When my voice does not reach clearly.

(Simple verse.)

Dagh-e dil gur nazar naheen aata
Bou bhi aye charagar naheen aati

If one can't see the burn-stained heart,
No smell too, my dear, does it impart.

(Another simple verse.)

Hum wahaan hain jehan say hum ko bhi
Kutch hamari khabar naheen aati

We are at such a spot from where, we our self,
Get to get no news, of our own self.

(Self explanatory verse.)

Murtae hain arzoo mein murnay ki
Mauth aati pur naheen aati

We face death in waiting for death.
Death comes near, but far away it is yet.

(The poet says he wants to sacrifice his life for the beloved. Death comes close in the form of separation from the loved one, which is worse than a physical death.)

Kabay kis munh say jaoo gay Ghalib
Sharam tum ko magar naheen aati

Ghalib, to Kaba how will you go?
When even remorse you do not have -- Lo!

(Simple and self contained verse.)

MILTEE HAI KHO E YAR SAY NAAR ILTEHAB MEIN

Miltee hai kho e yar say naar, iltehaab mein
Kafir hoon, gar neh miltee hoe rahat aazab mein

Resembles my beloved's nature, the fire, in fury and rage.
Would be lying were I to say, I get no pleasure, in such stage.

(The beloved's demeanour resembles the fury of fire, but this virulent nature is what is pleasing to the poet.)

Kab say hoon, qaya bataoon, jehan e kharab mein
Shub hayae hijr ko bhee rakhoon gar hisaab mein

For how long, should I say, that I have been in this wretched world?
Were I to count too the duration, of blessed separation's eve, as it unfurled

(How long I have lived in this state of trouble and torture, is difficult to say. The number of days in themselves are hard to count, but the length of the night of separation is even beyond calculation.)

Ta phir, na intezar mein, neend ayae umar bhar
Aanay ka eahad kar gayae, ayae jo khawab mein.

Then in waiting, no sleep can come, till life's very end.
Promised to visit once, when in my dream, she did descend.

(Simple verse does not need explanation)

Qasid kay aatay aatay , khat eak aur likh rakhoon
Main janta hoon, jo woh likhaingay jawab mein.

Let me write another letter while waiting for the carrier's turn.
Although I know, what reply to it, she will send, in its return.

(Although the poet knows that the beloved will reject his overtures of love, yet he wants to write another love letter before the harbinger comes his way.)

Mujh tak, kab un ki bazam mein, aata tha daur e jam
Saqi nay kutch mila neh diya hoe sharab mein.

When did the drink ever reach me, in their feast.
The saqi may have tampered the wine, and was certainly indiscreet.

(Rather easy to comprehend.)

Joe munkiar e wafa hoe, faraib ous pay qaya chalay
Qayoon badguman hoon doost say dushman kay baab mein

One that rejects faithfulness, cannot be fooled with devotional lies.
Why then, doubt a friend, for the sake of an enemy's guise.

(A person who refuses to be faithful can not understand the language of devotion and love. An enemy should thus not be confused for a friend.)

Main muztarab hoon wasal mein khoof e raqeeb say
Dala hai tum ko veham nay, kis peach o taab mein

At the moment of fulfilment, i worry about the rival and his deceit.
What thoughts of doubt, come and confuse you, - oh! my sweet?

(Self explanatory verse.)

Hai taveri charhee huyee andar naqaab kay
Hai eak shikan paree huyee turfaay naqaab mein

Puckered though the brow is in the all enclosing veil,
A slight crease in the cloth of it, however, tells the tale.

(Simple and quite clear.)

Main aur khitta e vassal, khudasaaz baat hai
Jaan nazr daynee bhool gaya isztaraab mein

Seeing myself, at the height of delight,-- to say the very truth.
I forgot to make the pledge of my life, -- how foolish and uncouth.

(The poet was so overjoyed to be at the peak of fulfilment of his wish, that he forgot to pledge his life and soul to the beloved.)

Lakhoon lagaoo, aik churana nigaah ka
Lakhoon banaoo, aik bigarnaa aataab mein

A thousand ways to show love, --one not to look in the eye.
A thousand ways to pretend, --One, just to let the temper fly.

(There a million ways to show acquaintance, one is to stealthily look away. Just like one way to pretend is fake anger and disapproval, although the heart may be jumping with joy.)

Voh naala, dil mein khass kay barabar jagaah neh payae
Jis naalay say shigaaf paray aaftaab mein

The sigh does not find, a speck of space, within her heart.
That which can however split, even the mighty sun, apart.

(The mystique of a sigh is that sometimes it does not even make the hard hearted love to raise an eye brow, but sometimes a sigh can split the sky.)

Voh sehar, muda-aa talabee mein neh kam aa yae
Jis sehar say safeena rawaan hoe saraab mein

That morn, will not   fulfill any desire, be it small or large.
On which, the caravan sets forth, for a journey in the mirage.

(It is a sorrowful and cursed time which does not fulfill a desire or at which a fateful journey makes a start.)

Ghalib chutee sharab per ab bhi kabhee kabhee
Peetaa hoon roz e abar shab e mahataab mein

Ghalib, though now I abstain from wine, its pleasure or delight.
Yet sometimes take a taste of it, on a cloudy day, or a moon lit night.

(A very simple and yet a beautiful verse.)

GHAM E DUNIYAN SAY GAR PAIYAE BHI FURSAT SIR UTHANAY KI

Gham e duniyan say gar paiye bhi fursat sir uthanay ki
Falak ka daikhna taqreeb tarey yaad anay ki

Even if there was a break, to lift the head from the worldly worries;
See the heavens reminder, of the scene of your forgotten memories.

(Whenever the poet gets a free moment from the chores of life, he is reminded of his beloved. He is complaining to heaven for not providing him any relief.)

Khulay ga kis tarah mazmoon meray maktoob ka ya rab
Qasam khai hai ous nay kaghaz kay jalanay ki

Oh Lord! How will the contents of my writings be known;
To destroy and burn the paper, the heretic has sworn.

(How can it be known what I wrote in the love letters, when the beloved is bent upon burning them as soon as she receives them.)

Lapatna parniyan main shoala e aatish ka aasan hai
Valay mushkil hai hikmat e dil main soza e gham chupany ki

It's easy to wrap up a flame In a flowery silken pelt.
The expertise, to hide the pain, of the sorrow of the heart, is but very difficult.

(The poet says it is relatively easy to cover an open flame under a cloth, but to hide the sorrow of the heart is not easy.)

Ounhain manzoor apnay zakhmioon ko daikh ana tha
Othay thay sair e gul ko daikhna shokhee bahanay ki

Their intent was to go and see, those inflicted by their ruse.
Got up to take a garden stroll, see the cleverness of excuse.

(The real idea was to go and see what was the condition of those who were rejected by the beloved. She, however, made an excuse as if she wanted to go and see the flowers in the garden.)

Humari saadgi thi iltafat e naz par marna
Tera ana tha zalim magar thameed janay ki

Our simplicity was to dote on her seductive charms.
But you came O' faithless one, to constantly,
remind of returning, and thus raise alarm.

(The poet was absorbed in the charms of the beloved who came to visit him. She, however, kept reminding him of her intent to leave soon and this kept him worried all the time and not fully enjoy the moments of infatuation.)

Lakad kob e havadis ka tahamul kar naheen sakti
Mare taqat ki zamin thee butoon kay naz uthanay ki

Lakad Kob: mar kutai
Havadis: hadsaat

A sting cannot wait, for the faithless blow to strike.
My strength, however, bore the brunt of the idol's might.

(The pain is rather in a hurry for the strike to fall, so that it may quickly show its effect. But the poet says he had immense strength to bear even the might of the idol's, meaning his beloved's, tortures.)

Kahoon kaya khoobey e auzaaye e ibnay zaman Ghalib
Badi ki ous nay jis say hum nay ki thee baraha naiki

What can Ghalib say about the traits, of the sons of the time.
Those we favoured, always repaid by ill will, For no reason or rhyme.

(Ghalib says that though he did not harm anyone yet the selfish people only repaid his kindness with unkindness.)

LATAFAT BAY KASAFAT JALWA PAIDA KAR NAHEEN SAKTI

Latafat bay kasafat jalwa paida kar naheen sakti
Chaman zangar hai aaina-e baday baharee ka

Pleasure without intensity, cannot enchantment bring.
The greenness of the garden, Mirrors the drunkenness of spring.

(To give pleasure there should be intensity and feeling in the act or the scene. The garden turns lush green on account of drunkenness, due to the intense beauty of the spring.)

Hareef-e joshish-e dariya naheen khudareeay sahil
Jehan saqi hoe too batil hai davaa hooshiaree ka

The serenity of the shore is not envious, of the restlessness of the sea.
Where yourself you, are the saqi; Untrue, would the claim to sobriety be.

(The sea shore is completely still and serene because it is fully laden and satisfied with the state it is in, much against the up and down and the restlessness of the ocean. The poet is just comparing the opposite moods of the two entities. In the next stanza of the verse he says that if the beloved is the one offering the drink, her own intoxicating beauty adds to the effect and it is impossible not to get drunk and to remain sober.)

LAZIM THA KEH DAYKHOO MERA RASTA KOI DIN AUR

Lazim tha keh daykhoo mera rasta koi din aur
Tanha gayay kayoon abb rahoo tanha koi din aur

Your were bound to have waited for me, yet you left before;
Why did you go alone? now be alone for some more.

(He is complaining to his departed friends, those who died before him, that since they could not wait for him here in this world they will have to wait for him there for his arrival.)

Mitt jayay ga sir gar tera pathar neh ghisay ga
Hoon dar pay tere naasia farsa koi din aur

The head will perish, but not your stone.
Short is my visit to your door, soon I will be gone.

(simple verse.)

Aayay ho kal aur khatay ho keh jaaoon
Mana keh haumaishaa nahin acha , koi din aur

Arrived just yesterday and today you say " I must go".
Agreed, always is not good, yet not so quick, as so.

(Simple verse.)

Jaatay huayay kehtay ho qaimat main millayan gay
Kaya khoob qaimat hai goya koi din aur

While departing you recon that, we will meet at the day of doom.
As if after now, for doom there is some more room.

(The time of departure of the beloved is the final doom for the poet. He can not recon another time as doom.)

Haan aay falk peer jawan tha abhi Arif
Qaya tera bigarta jo neh marta koi din aur.

Yes! Lord of heaven the pious one was still in his youth.
What would you have lost, were he not yet to taste death.

(Ghalib had lost a loving nephew when he was still a young man. This devastated him and thus the lament to heaven for taking him away so soon.)

Tum mah e shab char daham thay meray ghar kay
Phir qyaoon neh raha ghar ka wooh naqasha koi din aur

You were a short lived glory In my house's dome.
Why did not the map remain the same of my home.

(Simple verse. Read in conjunction with the previous verse to get the context.)

Tum kaoon say thay aaysay kharay dad o satad day
Karata malak ul maut taqaza koi din aur

How come you were so forthright In your deals?
The angle of death could have waited for his meals.

(Simple verse.)

Mujh say thumain nafrat sahee nayyar say laraee
Bachoon ka bhee daykha neh tamasha koi din aur

Admitted that you hated me and despised (your wife) the morning star;
You did not wait enough for the off springs too, by far.

(Read with reference to the context of the previous verses.)

Guzaree neh bahar haal yeh mudat khoosh o nakhoosh
Karna tha jawan marg guzara koi din aur

This duration somehow passed, happily or sad.
Oh! Youthful death, more endurance you should have had.

(Ghalib says that the time passes some way or the other. However, it would have been better if you had not died in young age.)

Nadaan hoe jo kehtay hoe qayoon jeetay hoe Ghalib
Kismet main hai marnay ki tamana koi dinn aur

You are novice to say, " why Ghalib still has breath" ?
It is destined that he should desire some more for his death.

(Self explanatory verse.)

MASJID KAY ZER E SAYA KHARABAAT CHAHIYAY

Masjid kay zer e saya kharabaat chahiyay
Bhooan pas aankh qibla e hajaat chahiyay

By the shadow of the mosque a tavern, -- there should be.
Brow near the eye, and, direction for wants, -- there should be.

(This is Ghalib's intricate philosophy where he correlates opposites to convey the meaning of things, and shows that pairs are essential to maintain a proper balance.)

Aashiq huyay hain aap bhi eik aur shaksh par
Aakhir sitam ki kutch to makafaat chahiyay

You too have fallen in love with another being.
After all some compensation for torture, -- there should be.

(The poet feels satisfaction at the beloved having fallen in love with someone, for then she will get to know the suffering which will act as a compensation to the lover's own torture of him.)

Dae daad aye falak dil e hasratparast ke
Haan kutch na kutch talafee e maafaat chahiyay

Oh! Heaven, praise the heart carrying so many unfulfilled desires.
Yes, some redress, for bygones, -- there should be.

(If heaven praises the poet for at least his steadfastness, it will somehow be a compensation for his unfulfilled desires.)

Sikhay hain mehrookhoon kay liayay hum musavarri
Taqreeb kutch to behr e mulaqaat chahiyay

We have taken up sketching, for moon-faced beauties.
Some occasion to meet them, -- there should be.

(A relatively simple verse which is self explanatory.)

Mai say gharaz nishat hai kis roosia ko
Eik goona bekhudi mujhay din raat chahiyay

Which wretched sinner seeks pleasure from wine.
A deep oblivion, day and night, for me, -- there should be.

(A simple yet very meaningful verse.)

Hai rang lala o gul e Nasreen juda juda
Har rang mein bahar ka asbaat chahiyay

The colours of red rose and narcissus are different.
Proofs of spring in every shade, -- there should be.

(Simple yet so philosophical a verse.)

Sir paa e khum pay chahiyay hangam e bekhudee
Roo suay Qibla waqat e manajaat chahiyay

At the place of wines, should be a sense of senselessness,
At the time of prayer, face towards the Qibla, -- there should be.

(Once again an emphasis on the difference of things and varied effects at different times. He says there should be all the fun and frolic at a party, but directed devotion and serenity on the spot of worship.)

Yanee bahisb e gardish e pamana e safaat
Arif humashaa musht e mai zaat chahiyay

Like the frequency of the cup's rotation measures the intensity of its service,
A saint always absorbed in selflessness, -- there should be.

(The cup seems to rotate faster as the drunkenness increases; hence the more saintly a person gets the more devoid of selfishness he should become.)

Nusho numa hai aasal say Ghalib farooh ko
Khamoshee he say niklay hai joo baat chahiyay

The branches feed and flourish from the stem –O' Ghalib.
Only which is spoken softly, that talk, -- there should be.

(The extremities all get nourishment from the stem. Softly spoken words gather strength from the subject matter of the topic.)

MUDAT HUI HAI YAR KO MEHMAN KIYAY HUAY

Muddat hui hai yar ko mehman kiyay huay
Josh-e qadah say bazam chiraghan kiyay huay

Its been an age, since my friend has guested with me.
And the twinkle of wine, has sparkled the company.

(This is simple and does not need further elaboration.)

Karta hoon jama phir jigar-e lakht lakht ko
Arsa hua hai davat-e mishgaan kiyay huay

Once again I gather, my shattered being, piece by piece.
Much time has fleeted since, upon those eye lashes, I did feast.

(The beloved has inflicted so much pain that the poets entire life has been shattered. The poet says that he is picking up its pieces and is then planning to face the beloved again, as it has been long since he saw her and fell victim to her killer glances.)

Phir waza-e ehtiaat say ruknay laga hai dum.
Barsoon huay hain chaak gariban kiyay huay.

Again, with the constraints of dignity, I have begun to suffocate.
Years have passed, since I let go, my pent up feeling's gate.

(This verse shows that worldly constrains have held the poet back. But now the intensity of desire to meet the beloved and speak his heart out leaves no room for such cares.)

Phir garm nala haay shararbar hai naffas
Muddat hui hai sair-e chiraghaan kiyay huay.

Then again, every breath complains and snorts out sparks of fire.
An age has lapsed, since I strolled, the well -lit rue of desire.

(A long time has passed since the poet has had a chance to take a walk along the glittering route where desires are fulfilled.)

Phir purshish-e jarahhat-e dil ko, chala hai ishq
Saman-e sad hazar, namakdan kiyay huay

Once again, love goes to enquire, about the wounds of the heart.
With a hundred thousand salt-shaker's, laden in its cart.

(It is love which gives the wound and pain to the heart. Here the poet portrays the sly nature of love. Though it goes to enquire about the well being of the heart, it deceitfully carries some salt. Intending to spread it on the wounds to bring back subdued memories.)

Phir bhar raha hoon khama-e mishgan ba khoon-e dil
Sazay chaman tarazeay daman kiyay huay

Once again, I fill the pen of her lashes, with the blood of my heart.
Carrying garden's enchantments,displayed in my shirt's front-part.

(Blood rushes in the veins the moment the poet sees those eye lashes. However, to see them he brings a lap full of flowers for his love.)

Baham digar huay hain, dil o deedah phir raqeeb
Nazara o khayal ka sammaan kiyay huay

The heart and sight have again, become each other's rival.
One set to view to the fullest, the other just desire,--on her arrival.

(The heart and sight are rivals in the sense that, upon seeing the beloved the power of the mind gets lost, and the lover cannot say the so many things his heart had planned. He is just lost in looking and admiration.)

Phir dil tawaf-e kouay malamat ko jayay hai
Pindar ka sanamkada weeran kiyay huay

Then again, the heart goes past the lover's abode.
Deserting the temple and idols, of its own imaginary code.

(The poet had planned never to visit the lover's lane after having been rebuked and insulted by her. But the intensity of love pushes him to go there and forces him to eat humble pie.)

Phir showq kar raha hai kharidar ki talab
Aarz -e Muta-e aqal o dil o jan kiyay huay

Once again the desire seeks and looks for a buyer.
With willingness to part with--sense, the heart, and life's own fire.

(This is another way of showing the intensity of love. The prize for the right buyer is all that the poet possesses -- his heart, sense and even life itself.)

Phir chahata hoon nama-e dildar khoolna
Jan nazar, dilfarabeeay unwaan kiyay huay

Over again, I want to open the letters she had sent.
Ready to sacrifice my life, on their heart rendering content.

(Self explanatory.)

Mangay hai phir kisi ko lab-e baam par havis
Zulfay siha rukh pay parishan kiyay huay

Once again, the greed of passion, wants someone on the balcony.
With the cascade of hair, flowing on her face, in melancholy.

(No need for further explanation.)

Chahay hai phir kisi ko muqabil mein aarzoo
Surmay say taez dashna-e mishgaan kiyay huay

Again, to be by my side, is my heartfelt desire.
Of one, whose lashes with the eye-liner, be like fire.

(Simple enough.)

Eik naubahar naz ko takay hai phir nigaah
Cherah faroogh e mai say gulistan kiyay huay

A blooming youth I search again, with these eyes of mine.
Whose face would glow, with the radiance of flowery wine.

(Quite self explanatory .)

Phir jee mein hai kay dar pay kisi kay paray rehain
Sir zerbar-e minat-e darban kiyay huay

This heart's desire is to take up station again, at someone's door.
Head bowed before the guard, and pleading -- 'Just! a little while more.'

(The poet is pleading for some more time at the beloved's door, in the hope he may catch her glimpse.)

Jee dhoondta hai phir wohee fursat kay raat din
Baithay rehain tasawar-e jana kiyay huay

The heart seeks once again, those lazy days and nights.
To sit around and dream, of the bygone blissful sights.

(Simple enough.)

Ghalib humain na chaaer kay phir josh-e ashkk say
Baithay hein hum thahaiya-e toofan kayay huay

Oh! Ghalib do not tease, for we are bent upon --
Shedding endless tears, to become a raging storm.

(The feelings are so pent up that if someone teases just a little, the poets weeping will bring about a storm, which may not stop easily.)

NA THA KUTCH TO KHUDA THA

Na tha kutch to Khuda tha Kutch na hoota to Khuda hoota
Dubooya mujh ko honay nay Na hoota main to kaya hoota

When naught existed, God existed. Had none there been, God would be.
My own existence lowered me. Would I not be, what would it be?

(Ghalib, like Plato and Pythagoras, projects the idea that man is fallen divinity. This is the meaning he projects in this verse. For a further elaboration see closing of my introduction to ' Ghalib as I understand him.'.)

Hua jub gham say yoon bayhiss To gham kaya sir kay katnay ka
Na hoota gar juda tan say To zanoon pay dhara hoota

When sorrow made it so insensitive,
why then the sorrow for a severed head?
For were it not separated from the body,
would have stayed reposed on the knees, instead.

(When too much sorrow turns the feelings insensitive, then one should not worry if the head is chopped off. For if it (head) feels dejected and is sad most of the time it hangs low in dejection and is not of much use anyway.)

Huyee mudatat kay Ghalib mar gaya Par yaad ata hai
Who har aik baat par khaina Kayh yoon hoota to kaya hoota

It's been an age since Ghalib passed away, yet,
we cannot but, remember and see;
The way, on every topic he would say, if it were so, how would it be?

(Ghalib is explaining his own temperament and approach to any subject, for he would question and enquire about the true nature of things.)

NAQSH FARYADEE HAI KIS KE SHOKHIAY TAHREER KA

Naqsh faryadee hai kiss ke shokhiay tahreer ka
Kaghazee hai pairahan her paikaray tasweer ka

Whose dazzling work, does the impression stricture.
Of paper is the robe, of every figure in the picture.

(This is the first verse of the first poem posted in Ghalib's 'divan' (collection of poems). The poet's thought process and the basis of his philosophy are reflected in it. The poet says that ' The impression' – 'the picture' or 'creation', is questioning, crying out loud, for having been given the brilliance and the joy of being created-- brought into existence and bestowed with the knowledge and consciousness of it. Yet there is lament and pain of awareness because all is temporary and short lived, just like the dress of paper of each figure face in the picture. This, in other words, is the question that humans ask of the Creator.)

Kavay kavay sakht jani hai tanhayee na pooch
Subh karna shaam ka lana hai jooyeh sheer ka

Trial upon trial, torture is life; Ah! of loneliness do not talk.
To go through the night till dawn, Is to dig a milk canal through a rock.

(Life is full of ups and downs, trials and tribulations at every stage, yet each individual has to go through it by himself, all alone. One cannot live anyone's life nor can another live for someone else. Each has to bear his own burden. So much so that even some thoughts cannot be shared with another, hence the feeling of extreme loneliness. Remember all heights are lonely and the more unique the idea the greater the feeling of isolation.)

Jazba e bay ikhtiaaray shooq dekha chahiyeh
Seenae shamsheer say bahir hai dam shamsheer ka

Watch the spirit of the untamed desire;
Beyond the chest, is the sword's own ire.

(A desire over which there is no control is akin to a sword whose sharpness is outside of it -- on its edge, not within the body where it may be harnessed or controlled.)

Agahee damay shuneedan jis qadar chahay bichaey
Mudda-ae unqua hai apnay alamay taqreer ka

Spread the sense of awareness to its ultimate extent.
Unique and rare is the topic of my sacrament.

(Here the poet says, however hard one may try to understand, grasp and master his poetry and its philosophy, it will be really difficult to do so for the subject matter he deals with is quite rare, obscure and unique.)

Buskay hoon Ghalib aseere may be aatish zaeray pa
Munh e aatish deeda hai halqa meri zangeer ka

Though incarcerated, O' Ghalib, yet have fire under my feet.
Each link of my fetter is like hair, curled with intense heat.

(Although man is imprisoned and cannot escape from the burden of life, yet he is always restless and keeps on trying—questioning and enquiring into the meaning of things. Each link of the chain of life seems to be formed out of hot metal that has curled up like a hair does with intense heat.)

RONAY SAY AUR ISHQ MAY BAYBAAK HOE GAYAY

Ronay say aur ishq may baybaak hoe gayay
Dhoay gayay hum aisay keh bus paak hoe gayay

Weeping in love made us fearless, further, all the more.
Were washed in such a way, that we became clean and pure.

(The poet being of eastern tradition believed in keeping his love under cover, but that he could not help weeping. This made him fearless and the catharsis of weeping has purified and cleansed his heart.)

Sarf e baha e mai huay aalaat e mai kashee
Thay yeh he doe hisab so yoon paak hoe gayay

So much wine flowed through, that, the drinking vessels too were washed away.
These were two accounts to settle, so they both went their way.

(The excessive drinking spell made even the vessels turn empty and roll over. Both the wine and the containers were consumed and empty. There will thus be neither pot nor broth.)

Rusva e dehar go huay awargee say tum
Barae tubiyatoon kay toe chalak hoe gayay

Though shunned by the world, on account of your aimlessness.
However, at least, you acquired cleverness and shamelessness.

(The poet is consoling the lady love, who is a singing and dancing girl and thus rather ill reputed, that it really does not matter if people call her names. Her over exposure to men has at least made her quite worldly wise.)

Kehta hai kaoon nala e bulbul ko bay asar
Parday main gul kay laakh jigar chaak hoe gayay

Who says the robin's cry has no feeling or effect.
Behind the cover of the rose a million hearts it did dissect.

(Simple verse.)

Puchay hai kaya wajood o adem ehail e shouq ka
Aap apni aag kay khas o khashaak hoe gayay

Oh! What do you enquire about life and death of those lost in desire.
Themselves, they became the fodder of the intensity of its fire.

(The intensity of desire is being compared to the fire which consumes the wood itself which provides it the material for burning in the first place.)

Kar nay gayay thay ous say taghaful ka hum gila
Ki eak he nigah keh bus khaak hoe gayay

Went there to complain about her manner unassumed.
She gave a single gaze and we were totally consumed.

(Simple verse.)

Iss rang say uthaee kal ous nay Asad ki naash
Dushman bhi jis ko daekh kay gamnaak hoe gayay

The other day she bore Asad's coffin in such a way.
That seeing it even the enemies were moved to dismay.

(simple verse.)

SATISHGAR HAI ZAHID ISS QADAR JIS BAGH E RIZWAN KA

Sataishgar hai zahid iss qadar jis baagh e rizvan ka
Who eik guldasta hai hum bekhudoon kay taaq e nusiyaan ka

The heavenly garden, whose endless praise the pious one sings.
Is but a bouquet in the niche, forgotten by us, the oblovious beings.

(Ghalib says that the pious one is most desirous of getting to heaven and devotes all his being to its attainment. He says that it seems to be just a pleasant thought that the likes of him have already left behind as just a dream and no reality.)

Na aayee saut e qatil bhee maana meray naloon ko
Liya dantoon main joe tinka hua resha nayistaan ka

Even the fury of the killer, could not subdue my wailing.
Every toothpick that I took turned soft, and limped away trailing.

(Even the fear of death could not intimidate the complaining of the poet. Every remedy he sought turned out to be ineffective.)

Dikhaoonga tamasha, dee agar fursat zamanay nay
Mera her daagh e dil eik tukham hai survey chiraghaan ka.

Will show a wonder, if the world gives me freedom.
Every stain of my heart, is but an egg of the burning sun.

(The poet says he too would have shown some lasting deeds if the worries of the world only gave him a chance. The stains of pain he carries are hot and burning like the off shoots of the sun.)

Kiya aaina khanay ka who naqsha teray jalway nay
Karay joe partave khursheed alam shabnamistan ka

The house of mirrors was shattered by your beauty, in many a ways.
Just as the sun light destructs, the dew's pretty face, by its rays.

(Simple verse.)

Maree tamer main hai muzhmir eik surat kharabee ke
Hewla burq e kharman ka, hai khoon e garm dehqaan ka

My construction has, a hidden defect from the start.
Husk along with grain, and warm blood of the farmer's heart.

(In the survival of one man is the labour and sacrifice of another, and each thing comes built-in with some form of negation and hindrance. just like the production of food requires the hard labour and sweat of the farmer.)

Ugaa hai ghar main her soo sabza, wiranee tamasha kar
Madaar ab khoodnay par ghaas kay hai mayray darbaan ka

Its green growth all around the house, desolation have fun.
The digging of the grass, now is the lot, of my guardian.

(Once again Ghalib points to a similar theme as the verse before. For he says that, although it is green all-around and desolateness is gone, yet now the poor gardener will have to labour to dig the grass.)

Khamooshi main nihaan khoongashta lakhoon aarzooian hain
Chiragh e murda hoon main bayzabaan goray gharibaan ka

Millions of bloods stain wishes, hidden in the silence be.
Like a burnt out lamp of a poor man's grave, Is, the tongue-tied me.

(The poet has very many unfulfilled desires and he bears the misery in silence, he burns out like a lamp by a poor man's tomb.)

Hanooz eik parteve naqsh e khayal e yar baqee hai
Dil e afsurda, goya hujra hai Yousaf kay zindan ka

For ever remains, the thought of love, like a shadowy impression.
The saddened heart is as if, a dungeon of Yousaf's prison.

(Yousuf or Joseph was locked up in prison in Egypt, and it is his sadness that the poet is depicting here.)

Baghal main ghair ke aaj aap sotay hain kaheen, warna
Sabab kaya khowab main aakar tabasum hai pinhaan ka

You sleep in the embrace of another, for otherwise,
What is the reason of coming in my dream, In such a smiling guise.

(simple verse.)

Naheen maloom kis kis ka lahoo pani hua hooga
Qaimat hai surshak aalooda hoona taree mishgan ka

Do not know how many bloods must have turned to water, O my dear.
Like dooms day is the scene, when your lashes get wet with tear.

(Simple verse.)

Nazar main hai hamari jada e rah e fana Ghalib
Keh yeh sheraaza hai aalam kay ajza e parishaan ka

In my sight O Ghalib, the way leading to freedom, is death.
That this is how the checker of the world, gets routed at its depth.

(Death is the only freedom when nothing seems to be going right. The way of the world is like a game of chess where all ends with the check and mate to the king.)

SUB KAHAN KUTCH LALA O GUL MEIN NUMAYAAN HO GAIYEEN

Sub kahan kutch lala o gul mein numayaan ho gaiyeen
Khaak mein kaya suratain hoon gee keh pinhaan ho gaiyeen

When have they all bloomed Into roses and flowery graces,
In the dust would be lost and hidden, so many faces.

(Ghalib says that the flowers and grasses in nature are all so beautiful, yet they are not enough to represent all the wonderful faces and things that have got buried in the earth over the ages.)

Yaad theen hum ko bhi ranga rang bazam arariyaan
Laykin ab naqash o nigar e taq e nusiyaan ho gaiyeen

To liven occasions we too had known, many sayings and speeches.
But now they are no more than lost decorations, in niches.

(The poet is lamenting the fact that in the past he too was a very lively person and the life of many a party, but the worldly woes have made him forget the fun and frolic.)

Theen binat ul naesh gardoon din kay purday mein nihaan
Shub ko oun kay jee mein kaya aayee keh urian ho gaiyeen

Daughters of the seven star galaxy were all enrobed by the day.
What entered their hearts at night, that they flung their garments away.

(A constellation of stars in Taurus is also known as the daughter of the Pleiades. They can obviously not be seen in the day. Ghalib describes this fact in his romantic imagination.)

Qaid mein Yaqoob nay lee goo na Yousaf ki khabar
Laykin aankhaan rozan e deevar e zindan hoe gaiyeen

Though Jacob did not enquire about Joseph, while in prison.
Yet his eyes turned stony, staring at the wall cracks of the dungeon.

(It is said that Jacob bore the days of separation from Joseph in silence and patience and that he lost his sight staring at the dungeon walls in his solitude.)

Sub raqeebon say hoon nakhush Pur zanan e misr say
Hai Zulaikha khush keh mehav e maah e Cunnan hoe gaiyeen

Am unhappy with all rivals, but with Egyptian women
Zulaikha is pleased that they, are entranced with the Cannan's moon.

(This is another religio- historic account, where it is said that Zulaikha who was infatuated by the beauty of Joseph called all her women friends and introduced them to him. She had given each lady a knife to peel the fruit being served at the time. When Joseph was called in and the women set their eyes on him, they were stupefied by his beauty and cut their hands instead of the fruit they were peeling. This vindicated her contention that Joseph's beauty was really electrifying. So Ghalib says that though I am unhappy with my rivals, Zulaikha was really pleased to see the state of her rivals upon exposure to the beauty of her love. Joseph who was also known as the moon of Cannan.)

Joo e khoon aankhoon say behnay doe keh hai sham e firaq
Mein yeh samjhoon ga keh shamaen doe firozan hoe gaiyeen

Let the eyes flow canals of blood, for it is the night of separation.
I will think as if two candles have been lit in preparation.

(Simple verse.)

In parizadoon say laingay khuld mein hum inteqaam.
Qudrat e Haq say yehee hoorain agar waan hoe gaiyeen

We will take revenge, from these fairy-types in heaven.
If by Nature's grace they come there, as houris given.

(Simple verse.)

Neend ous ke hai dimagh ous ka hai raataan ous ke hain
Taree zulfain jis kay bazoo par parishaan hoe gaiyeen

Sleep is her's, mind too, and the night also;
Your cascade upon whose shoulder fall and spread such and so.

(Simple verse, describes the height of infatuated imagination.)

Main chaman mein kaya gaiya goya dabistaan khul gaiya
Bulbulain sun kar meray naalay ghazalkhaan hoe gaiyeen

Just as I stepped in the park, as if a school's door flung open;
The robins, on hearing my lamantations, began reciting poems.

(Simple verse.)

Who nighaayan kayoon hui jatee hain ya rab dil kay paar
Jo meraee kotaeay qismat say mishgaan hoe gaiyeen

Why do, Oh! lord, those eyes pierce my heart in flashes.
Those, which to my misfortune, went under cover of the eye lashes.

(The beloved gave one glance and then lowered her eyes. The impression of that single glance was enough to send the poet into a trance of imagination and longing for more.)

Bus kay rooka main nay or seenay mein obhreen pay ba pay
Maree aahayaan bakhia e chaak e garibaan hoe gaiyeen

Now as I restrained them, they rose layer upon layer.
My cries of pain became the stitches of my open collar.

(The more the poet tries to restrain the feelings in his chest, the more they rise. So much so that being unable to escape, the sighs become like stitches that hold back his open and unrestrained collar.)

Waan gaya bhi main toe ous ke galiyoon ka kaya javaab
Yaad theen jitnee duaayaan saraf e darbaan hoe gaiyeen

Even if I go there, how will I face her disregard.
All prayers I knew were spent, to mould her portal-guard.

(Simple verse.)

Janfizaa hai bada jis kay haath mein jaam aagaya
Sub lakerein haath ke goya rag e jaan hoe gaiyeen

So pleasing is wine, that whoever handles a drink;
Feels his palm lines turn to veins full of life to the brink.

(Wine is so good in its effect, that when one picks up a glass, the lines of the palm all seem to come alive with the rush of blood.)

Hum muwahid hain humara caish hai tarkay rusoom
Millatain jub mitt gaiyeen ajzaa e imaan hoe gaiyeen

We are monotheists, our belief is to shun traditions and scribes.
Ingredients of faith flourish with the elimination of sects and tribes.

(Ghalib says that to be a pure monotheist one has to do away with factions and tribes.)

Ranj say khoogar hua insaan to mitt jata hai ranj
Mushkilain mujh pur pareen itnee keh aasan hoe gaiyeen

If man gets used to pain, it loses its bite and tease.
Yet I, suffered so much, that pain changed to ease.

(Here Ghalib says that if sadness perpetuates one gets used to it and becomes immune. But, he suffered even beyond that limit, and to an extent when sadness changed its very nature and started giving him pleasure.)

Yoon he gar roota raha Ghalib to aay ehlay jehan
Daikhna in bastion ko tum kay viraan hoe gaiyeen

If Ghalib goes on weeping in this way, then O! you worldly ones;
Just watch these dwellings go desolate, and turn to ruins.

(Here the poet says that he feels for the poor and weeps for them, but if nothing is done to alleviate human suffering all things will perish and die.)

TASKEEN KO HUM NA ROAYAN JOE ZOAQ E NAZAR MILAY

Taskeen ko hum na roayan joe zoaq e nazar milay
Hooran e khuld mein taree surat magar milay

We wouldn't cry for bliss, were the eye to get satisfaction.
Even though, your face matches the houris's, in perfection.

(The poet says that he has been looking for the fulfillment of his taste. Although the beloved's face is no less than that of a houris' (the maidens of heaven) in beauty, yet his desire for perfection is not satisfied.)

Apani gali mein mujh ko na kar dafan baad e qatal
Meray patay say khalq ko qayoon tera ghar milay

Having murdered, do not bury me in your lane.
Why from my resting place, should the world know, your name.

(Simple verse does not need elaboration.)

Saqi gari ki sharm karo aaj warna hum
Her shub pia he cartay hain mae jis qadar milay

For the saqi's sake, today, do stay away.
For otherwise we drink as much as we get, every single day.

(The poet is reprimanding himself for being desirous for a drink and says for the sake of the Saqi's (the drink serving hostess), he should restrain himself at least that day.)

Tujh say toe kutch kalam nahin lakin aay nadeem
Mera salam khaiyo agar nama barr milay

To you I have not much to say, O' friend, yet,
give my regards to the messenger, if on the way, you and he met.

(The poet is asking his friend in a polite way to enquire from the messenger if there is a letter to be delivered to Ghalib, who is patiently waiting for one.)

Tum ko bhi hum dikhayan keh Majnoon nay qaya kiya
Fursat kashakesh e gham e pinhann say gar milay

We could show you, what all was done by Majnoon;
If freedom we receive, from this hidden, painful doom.

(The poet says he too can excel Majnoon (the famous lover of Laila), if only he gets time from the worries of the world.)

Lazim naheen kay khizar ki hum paravee karayan
Maana keh eik buzurg humain haumsafar milay

It is not essential that, we should follow and abide;
Although, we had the company of an old and holy guide.

(It is not necessary to follow the advise of every senior and holy person, however pious he may be.)

Aye sakinan e kucha e dildar daykhana
Tum ko kahin jo Ghalib aashufta sir milay

Keep watch O' residents of the lover's lane.
May it be you come across, Ghalib! the insane.

(Simple verse.)

YEH NA THI HAMARI QISMAT KAY VISAL E YAR HOOTA

Yeh na thi hamari qismat kay visal e yar hoota
Agar aur jitay rehtay yehehi intezar hoota

It was not our destiny, to meet the sweet beloved.
If more we were to live, even longer would have waited.

(Simple verse does not need much explanation.)

Teray waday par jeeyay hum toe yeh jan jhoot jana
Keh khushi say mer na jatay agar aetebaar hoota

We lived by your promise; yet knew well that it was untrue.
We would have died of bliss, If in it we had faith too.

(The poet passed his entire life on the promises made by the beloved, though, he know that it was not true in the first place. He says if he had believed in the truthfulness of the promise he may well have died of happiness and joy.)

Taree nazuki say jana kay bundha tha eahed e booda
Kubhee tou na toarsakta agar istawaar hoota

Due to your frailty my dear, the knot was tied so subtle.
Never could you have severed it, had it but been brutal.

(The poet says that since the beloved was delicate the knots he tied too were frail. Had the tied knots been strong she would never have been able to break them.)

Koi mayray dil say poochay tarey teer e neem kash ko
Yeh khalish kahaan say hooti joe jigar kay paar hoota

Let some one enquire from my heart, about your half-drawn arrow.
Had it passed through and through, there would be no pain or sorrow.

(The beloved is supposedly firing arrows by her glances at the lover. He says that they would not be so hurtful if the glances were clear and unhesitant looks of love, for then he would perhaps not suffer so much.)

Rag e sang say tapakta who lahoo kay phir na thamta
Jisay gham sumajh rahay ho who agar sharaar hoota

The veins of stone would have shed blood unending;
What you think as sorrow had it been fire unbending.

(The hurt is ever so great, yet had the torture been more severe, even the veins of stone would have shed blood in their tears.)

Gham agarchay jaan gasal hai peh khaan bachaan keh dil hai
Gham e ishq gar na hoota gham e roozgar hoota

Though sorrow is life threatening, but, after all, the heart gets hurled.
Had there not been the pain of love, there would be worry of the world.

(The poet says that although the pain is severe yet one has no control over the heart and infatuation. For, he says, that if there were no pain and torture of love there would be the worldly woes.)

Kehhoon kis say mein kay kaya hai shab e gham buri bala hai
Mujhay kaya bura tha murna agar eik baar hoota

To who can I say what it is? the night of sorrow is a terrible thing.
I'd go willingly, if death came just once, not with repeated sting.

(The night of separation comes off and on and each time it is a terrible feeling like the suffering of death. He says he would not mind bearing it once but not repeatedly, for true death will come only once.)

Huay mur kay hum joe ruswa huay kayoon na garq dariya
Na khabi janaza uthta na kaheen mazar hoota

Why did we get ignominy in death? were not drowned instead.
There would not be a burial, nor a grave for eternal bed.

(Simple yet so meaningful.)

Usay koan deakh sakta keh yagana hai who yakta
Joe dueeyee ki bou bhi hooti to khain doe chaar hoota

Who can see Him? He is the One, the Most Unique.
So much as thought of duality, would make Him humble and weak.

(Here the poet is describing God and says one can not draw any inference about Him as He is unique, but, had there been another like Him, He too would be fathomable and weak.)

Yeh masail e tasavoof yeh tera bayaan Ghalib
Tujhay hum wali sumhajtay joe na badah khawaar hoota

This intricate philosophy O' Ghalib, and what a diction.
We'd consider you a saint, were it not for wine's addiction.

(This verse shows how Ghalib could detach and see even his own self so clearly, without any inhibitions or misgivings about his actions.)

YAK ZARRA E ZAMIN NAHEEN BAYKAAR BAAGH KA

Yak zarra e zmin naheen baykaar, baagh ka
Yan jadah bhee fateelah hai lalay kay daagh ka

Fateelah= chiragh ki batee
Lala= Eik lal phool jis kay andar kala dagh hota hai

Not even a speck of space, is useless, in the garden by far.
Even the footpath here, is a skin of the stamen of the red flower.

(Simple verse does not need elaboration.)

Bay mai kisay hai taqat, ashoob e agahee
Khaincha hai ijzz e hawsalaa nay, khutt ayaagh ka

Ashoob= shour, ghul
Ijzz= Kamzoree, shakist
Ayaagh= Piyala Jaam

Without wine, who has the strength, to bear the din of consciousness.
The defeat of courage has left a mark, on the rim's smooth evenness.

(When awareness and consciouness become acute it is difficult to find escape and only some intoxication preserves sanity. However, if courage and will power is lost one becomes an edict and a drunkard. Ghalib is emphasising the need to keep a balance in all acts.)

Bulbul kay karobaar peh hain, khandaa haayay gul
Kheytay hain jis ko ishqq, khalal hai dimagh ka

At the robin's doting -- Ah!, the flowers all laugh in jestation.
What they call love, is a figment of one's imagination.

(The flowers of the garden jest and laugh at the love and doting of the robin, who gets infatuated and sings merrily in the beauty of the spring. They all laugh because they know that this state of affairs is only temporary and short lived and will soon go away, and then the robin will have to come to grips with reality and once again get absorbed in the mundane search and labour for food and sheer survival.)

Taza naheen hai nasha e fikar e sukhan mujhay
Taryakee a qadeem hoon, dood e chiragh ka

My intoxicating love for poem and verse, is nothing new,
Am an old addict, to the fumes of the burning lamp, too.

(Fumes of the burning lamp go to show the fact that the poet is used to lonely nights by the lamp where he thinks and meditates and composes his verse and poems.)

Soo bar bund e ishqq say, aazad hum huayay
Pur kaya kuraayn keh dil hee udoo hai, firagh ka

A hundred times, the bonds of love, did even set us free.
But pray what's to do if, the heart detests freedom and liberty.

(Here the poet is portraying his feeling and deep love for incarceration and longing to be caged in the love of the beloved.)

Bay khoon e dil hai, chashamm main mauj e nigahh ghubaar
Yeh maikada kharaab hai, mai kay suraagh ka

Even without heart's blood in it, the eye tends to see things hazy.
Bad is this tavern, to give away the clue, by its lingering smell so crazy.

(The saddened hazy eyes do not need to see, the tavern's radiant smell is enough to give the clue of its location.)

Bagh e shaguftah teyra, bisaat e nishat e dil
Abrr e bahar, khumkada kis kay dimagh ka

The blooming garden is – but a spread of your heart's fascination.
The cloud of the monsoon -- a tavern's mist -- of whose imagination?

(The poet is saying that the clouds are like the mist of the tavern. It may well be the imagination of someone, Whose? It can not be said.)

ZIKR OUS PARI WESH KA

Zikr ous pari wesh ka aur phir bayaan apna
Bun gaya raqeeb aakhir tha joe raazdan apna

Description of that 'fairy type' and topped with our narration;
Our own confidant became a rival for her admiration.

(The poet says his description of the beauty of his own love was such that his own friend and confidant became his rival after hearing it.)

Main wooh kuyoon bohat peetay, bazam e ghair main ya rab
Aaj he hua manzoor oun ko imtehaan apna

Why, at a strangers feast, did they have to drink so much?
Just today they had to test their own ability – as such.

(Simple verse to comprehend)

Manzar eik blandi per aur, hum bana saktay
Arsh say idhar hoota kashkeh makan apna

We would have built another scene, at a lofty height.
If, only away from the sky, we could find a place or site.

(The poet says he would have built a much better world at a much higher level of standards, only if he could somehow escape the boundaries and the clutches of the heavens above.)

Dey wooh jis qadar zilat hum hansee main talaingay
Baray ashanaa nikla oun ka pasbaan apna

However much she may insult, we won't take it to heart.
For after all, her caretaker is a friend of ours, from the start.

(Relatively easy verse.)

Dard e dil likhoon kab tak, jaoon oun ko dikhlaoon
Oungliaan figar apni, khamah khoon chikan apna

How long should I write the sorrows of my heart,
why not go to her and show;
My severed fingers and the pen, which writes with the blood that flow.

(Writing up the endless sorrows of the heard has made his fingers bleed, and the blood has now become the ink with which he continues to inscribe.)

Ghistay ghistay mitt jaata, aap nay abas badla.
Nang e sijda say meray, sang e aastaan apna

Would itself have perished, there was hardly need to replace;
By the endless rubbing of my head, the sill of stone at your door's place.

(The poet says there was hardly need to replace the stone mat at the door, for by the constant rubbing of his forehead it would have vanished anyway.)

Takaray neh ghamazee, kar liya hai dushman ko
Dost ki shikayat main hum nay haumzuban apna

See how by complaining and backbiting, we have convinced even the enemy;
To be on our side, against one who was once so friendly.

(The poet says that his verbosity and tactful complaints has turned even the rival against the love of his beloved.)

Hum kehan kay daana they kis hunar main yakta they
Bay subab hua Ghalib dushman aasman apna

Not endless wisdom did we have, In which field did we excel?
For what reason, O Ghalib, then heaven's jealousies did swell.

(Rather simple verse.)

ZULMATKADAY MEIN MERAY SHAB E GHAM KA JOOSH HAI

Zulmatkaday mein meray shab e gham ka joosh hai
Eik shama hai daleel e sehrr so khamoosh hai

In my dark room is the reign of the sorrowful night.
The only evidence of morn, though silent, Is but the candles light.

(This is quite a self explanatory verse. Needs no further elaboration).

Nay mazhdah e visaal neh nazara e jamal
Muddat houi keh ashati e chasham o goosh hai

No good tidings of meeting, no view of the beautiful bearing.
Been long since friendliness was shown, by the sight and the hearing.

(The poet is quite dejected as there seems to be no news about the meeting with the beloved and no hope to see her face to face and talk. It has been a long time since luck favoured him).

Mai nay kia hai husan e khudara ko bay hijaab
Aay shouq haan ijazaat e tasleem o housh hai

Wine has lifted the veil, of the conceited beauty's tide
O! desire, yes, permission is granted to acclaim,
but with the rules must yet abide.

The effect of wine has been to give courage and lift the veil of the beloved's face. But only to admire the beauty, and to admire within limits of decency and tradition).

Gohar ko uqday gardan e khooban mein daeikhna
Qaya ouaj per sitara e goharfaroosh hai

See the bejeweled necklaces, caressing the beautiful necks.
What height does the star of the jeweler's luck begets.

The beauty of the jewel is itself enhanced by its display on the slender necks of the beautiful people. This in itself is enough reward for the jeweler's workmanship).

Deedar bada hawsalah saqi nigah e must
Bazam e khayal mekada e bay kharoosh hai

Drunkenness affords courage, to behold the saqi's intoxicating sight.
For otherwise the tavern of thought, Is without spark of delight.

Drunkenness promotes the sense of courage to enjoy the feelings and thoughts inhibited by the induced sobriety of traditions and culture. Only then the full flavour and enjoyment of the scene can by enjoyed).

Dekhoo mujhay joe deeda e ibrat nigha hoe
Maree sunoo joe gosh e nasihat nioush hai

Look at me if you have discerning eyes to see.
Give me full ear, To grasp advise from me.

(Simple logic and diction. Needs no further elaboration).

Saqi bajalwa dushmanay iman o aagahee
Mutrab zenaghma rahzan e tamkeen o hoosh hai

The saqi full of radiance, is enemy of faith and conscience.
Like the singer's sweet song is highway man of strength and sense.

(The saqi's (beautiful hostess who pours wines from decanters) enchanting beauty is provoking and enticing, adding fuel to the fire to the effect of wine, just as also is the sweet voice and song of the singer that makes one enjoy the intoxication even more).

Lutff e haram e saqi wa zauq e sadaiye chung
Yeh janat e nigah who firdaus e goosh hai

The pleasure of the saqi's drink, and the violin's enchanting sound.
This a paradise for the sight, that a heaven all around.

(The poet is just strengthening the meaning of the previous stanza and describing the feeling of pleasure and enjoyment of wine combined with music.)

Ya subhodum joe daykhiayay aakar to buzm mein
Nay who suroor o sooaz na josh o kharoosh hai

Or if you were to pass by the tavern In the morn.
Left there is no rhythm, and the sparkle too is gone.

(The poet is comparing the effect of the changing times on the person's moods and feelings).

Daag e firaq e sohabat e shab ki jalee hui
Eik shama rehgayee hai so voh bhi khamoosh hai.

Burnt up in the quest for night's commune and laden with its stains.
A candle, but it too silent, is all that remains.

(The scene of the next morning after having waited all night for the lady love is like the stains the candle has dropped on the floor. Having burnt all night in waiting silently and expectantly).

Aatay hain ghaib say yeh mazameen kahayal mein
Ghalib sareer e khama nawa e saroosh hai

These topics in the mind are of heavenly descent
Ghalib is sound of the moving pen and voice of angles sent.

(This verse describes the poet's depth of devotion and feelings which seem to prompt and motivate him in his poetry).